RECORDED VERSIONS GUITAR

AUTHENTIC TRANSCRIPTIONS
WITH NOTES AND TABLATURE

KEITH URBAN
Guitar Anthology

Cover photo by ZUMA Press, Inc / Alamy

Music transcriptions by Pete Billmann, Jeff Jacobson, Paul Pappas,
David Stocker, and Martin Shellard

ISBN 978-1-4803-6897-2

HAL•LEONARD®
CORPORATION
7777 W. BLUEMOUND RD. P.O. BOX 13819 MILWAUKEE, WI 53213

Visit Hal Leonard Online at
www.halleonard.com

Contents

from *Be Here*

Better Life

Words and Music by Richard Marx and Keith Urban

Drop D tuning:
(low to high) D-A-D-G-B-E

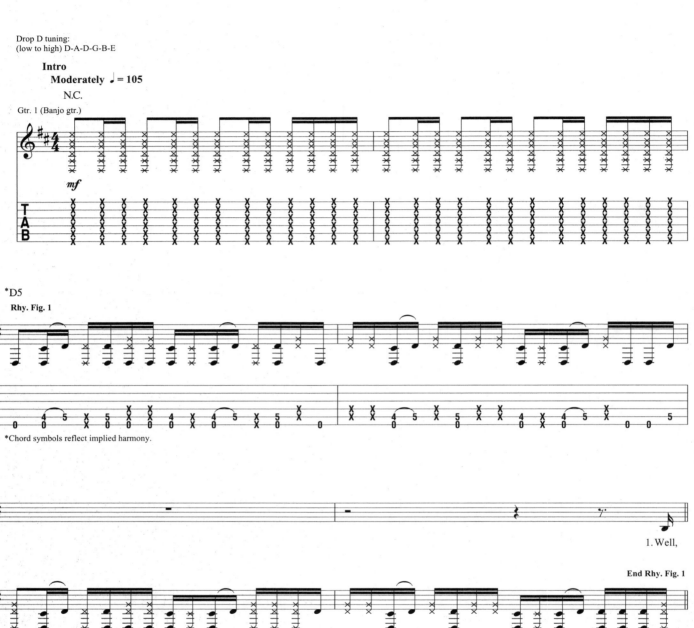

*Chord symbols reflect implied harmony.

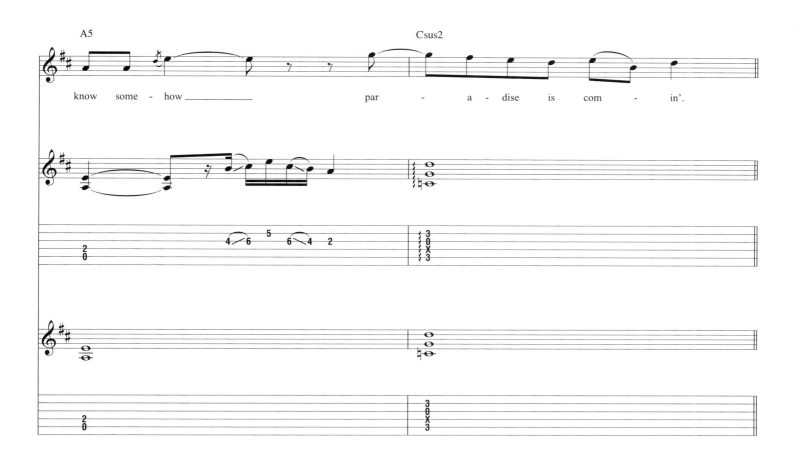

Chorus

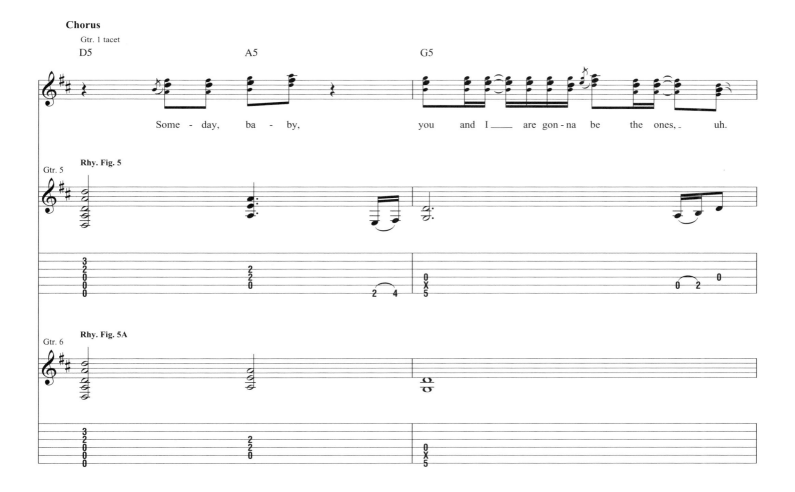

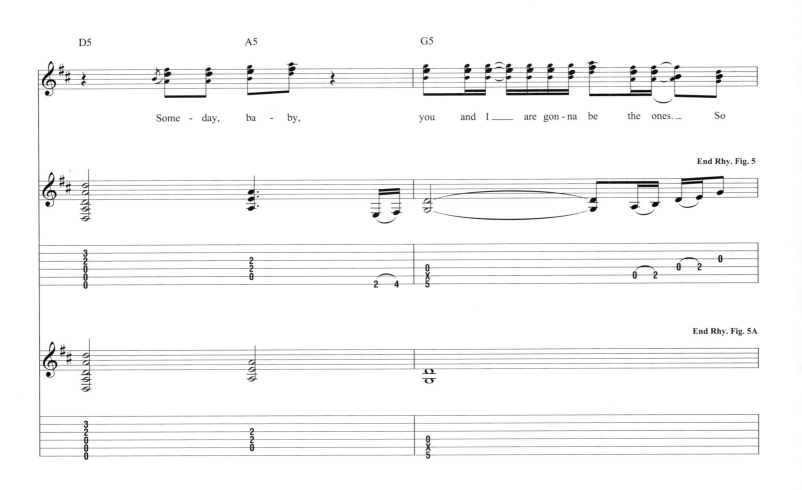

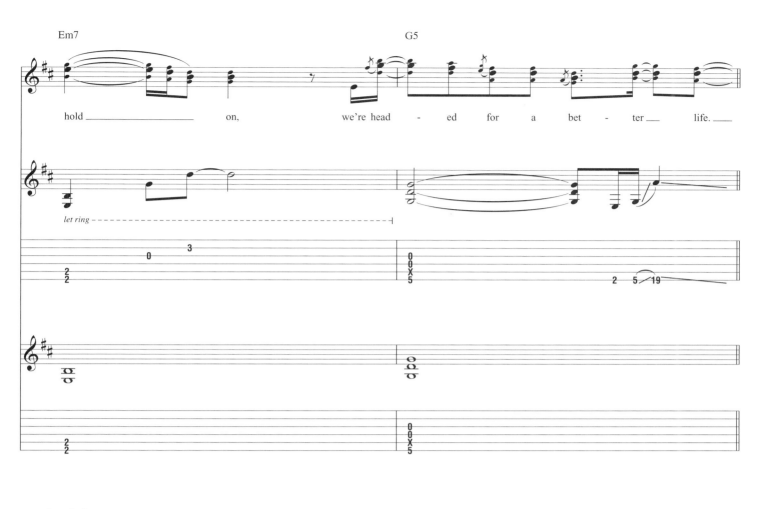

hold _____ on, we're head - ed for a bet - ter ___ life. ___

Interlude

Gtr. 1: w/ Rhy. Fig. 1

D5

Mm, hmm, _ hmm. 2. Oh, _ now, _

Gtrs. 5 & 6

pp

Verse

Gtr. 1: w/ Rhy. Fig. 2
Gtr. 4: w/ Rhy. Fig. 4

G5

there's a place ___ for you and me ___ where we can dream ___ as big as the sky, ___

yeah,   yeah. ___   I

know it's   hard __   to   see it   now, _   but, ba - by, some - day   you   gon - na ___

fly. ___   This

Pre-Chorus

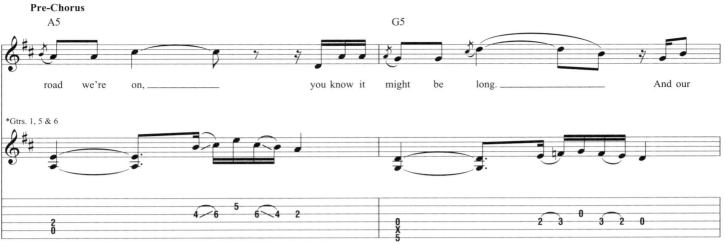

road we're on, _____ you know it might be long. _____ And our

*Gtrs. 1, 5 & 6

*Composite arrangement

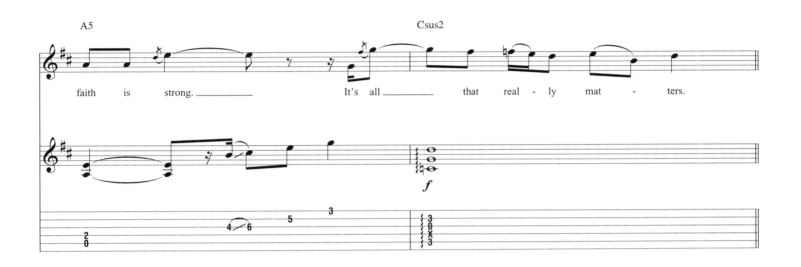

faith is strong. _____ It's all _____ that real - ly mat - ters.

Chorus
Gtr. 1 tacet
Gtrs. 5 & 6: w/ Rhy. Figs. 5 & 5A

Some - day, ba - by, you and I ____ are gon - na be the ones, ___ uh.

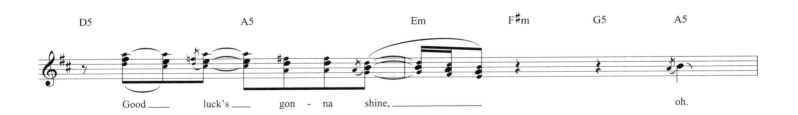

Good ____ luck's ____ gon - na shine, _____ oh.

Some - day, ba - by, you and I ____ are gon - na be the ones. ___ So

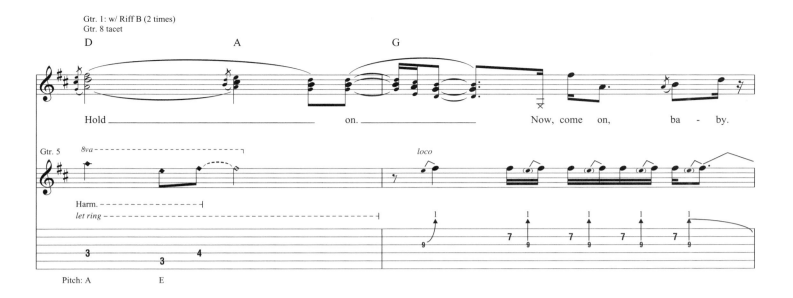

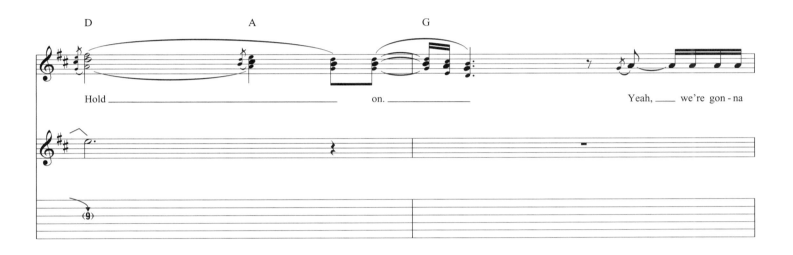

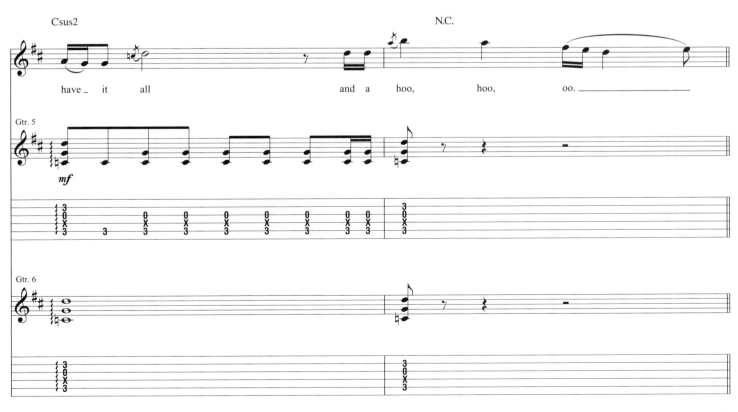

Chorus

Outro

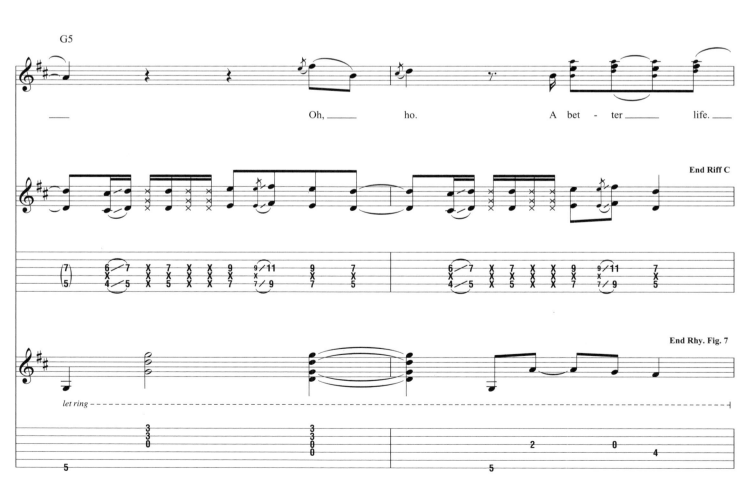

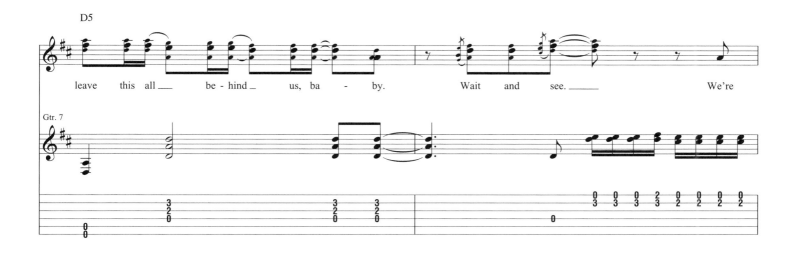

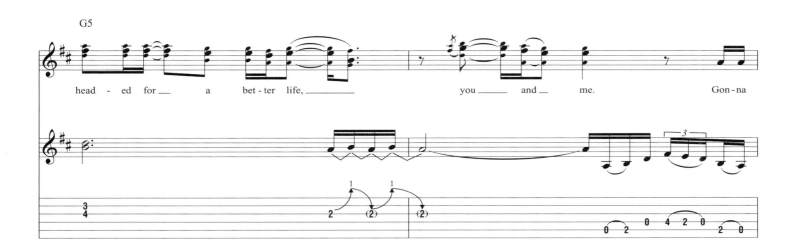

Gtrs. 5 & 6 tacet

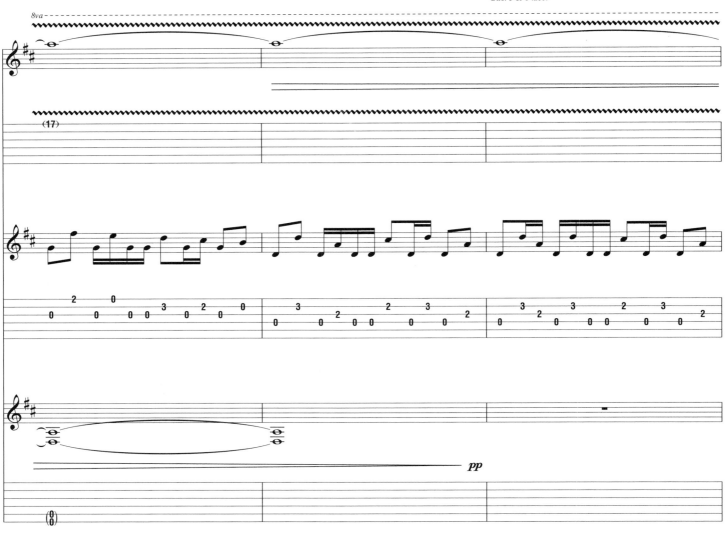

from *In the Ranch*

Clutterbilly

Words and Music by Keith Urban, Peter Clarke and Gregory Holden

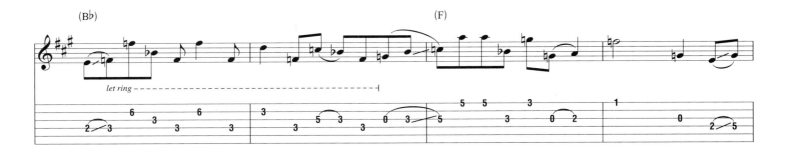

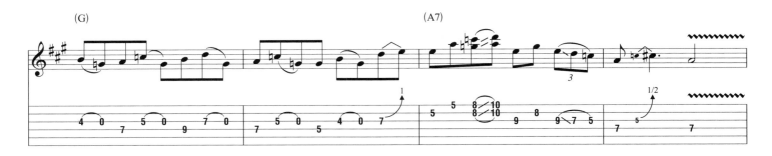

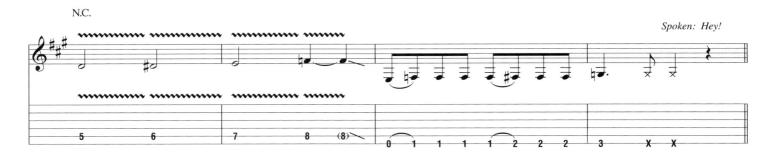

F

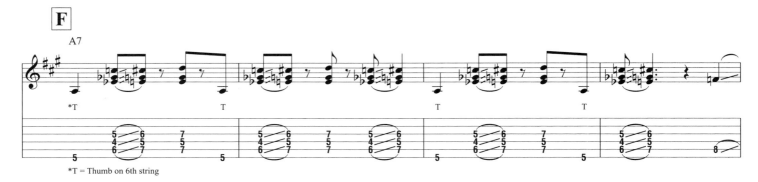

*T = Thumb on 6th string

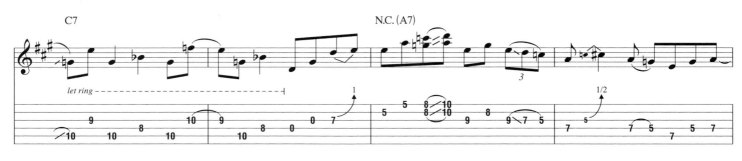

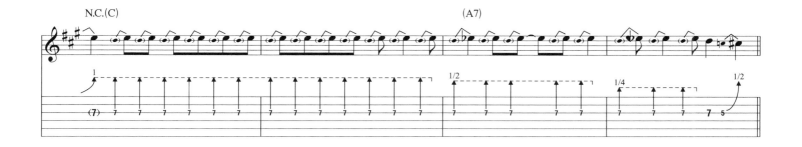

G

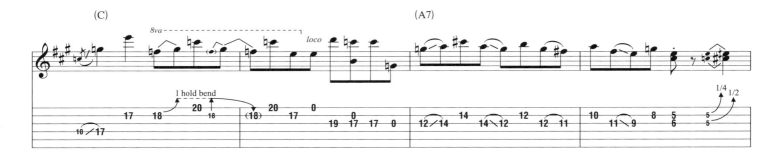

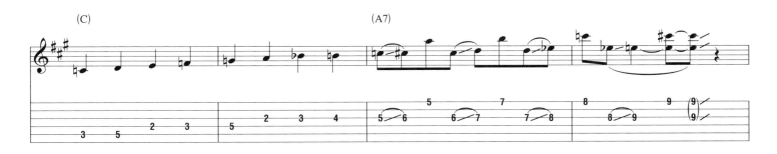

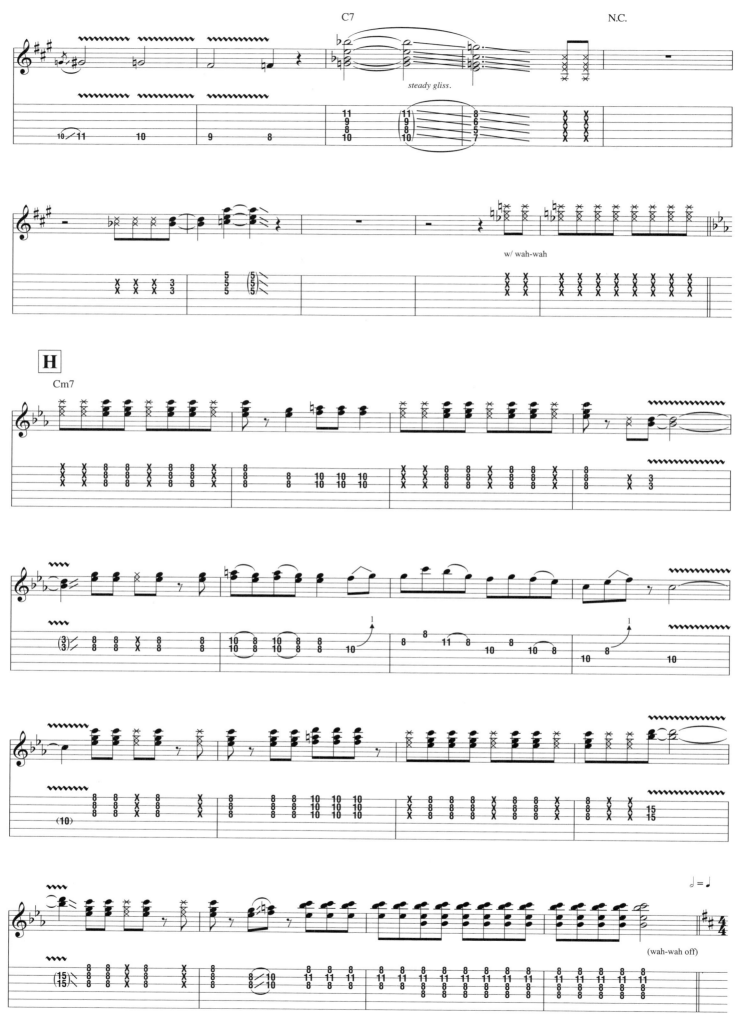

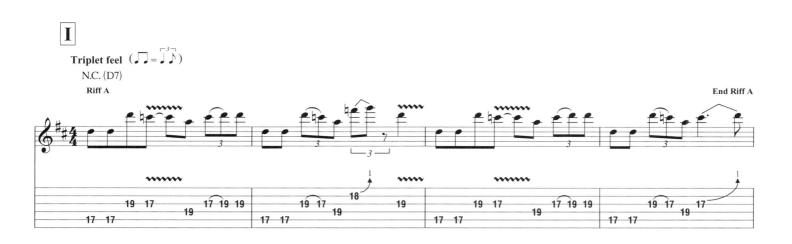

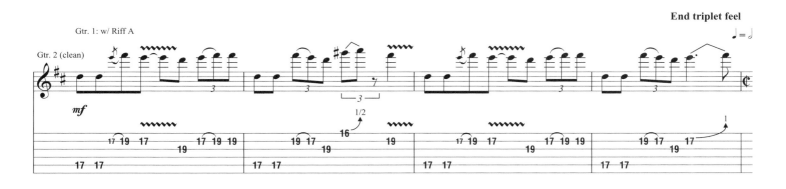

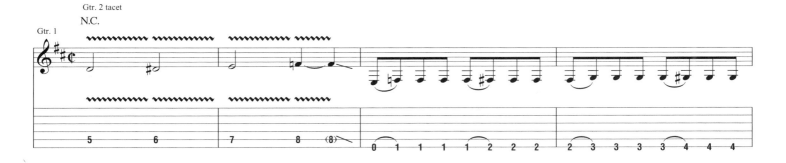

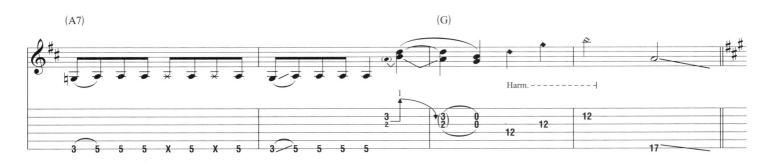

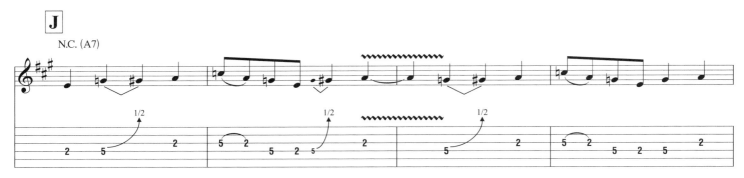

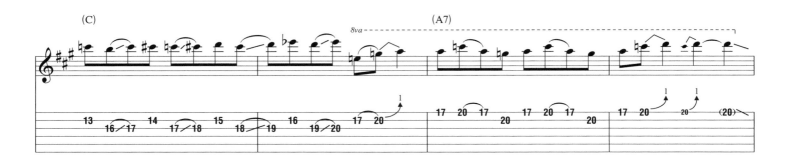

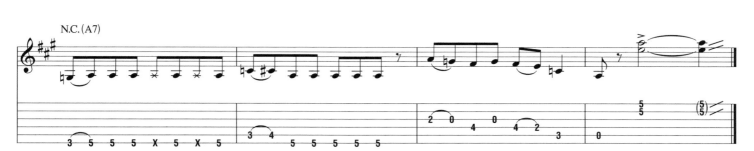

from *Be Here*

Days Go By

Words and Music by Monty Powell and Keith Urban

Gtr. 1: Capo VII

Gtrs. 2, 3 & 4: Drop D tuning:
(low to high) D-A-D-G-B-E

Intro
Rubato ♩ = approx. 98

*Symbols in parentheses represent chord names respective to capoed guitar.
Symbols above reflect actual sounding chords. Capoed fret is "0" in tab.

Moderately fast ♩ = 132

*Chord symbols reflect overall harmony.

Interlude

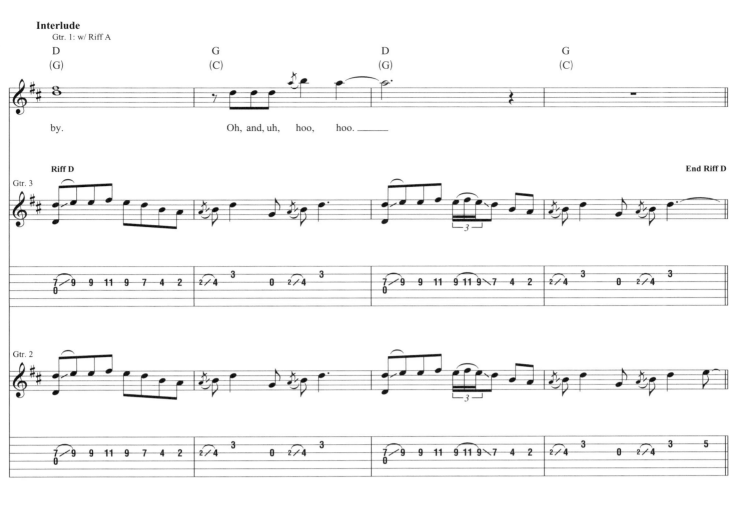

by.

Oh, and, uh, hoo, hoo. _____

Verse

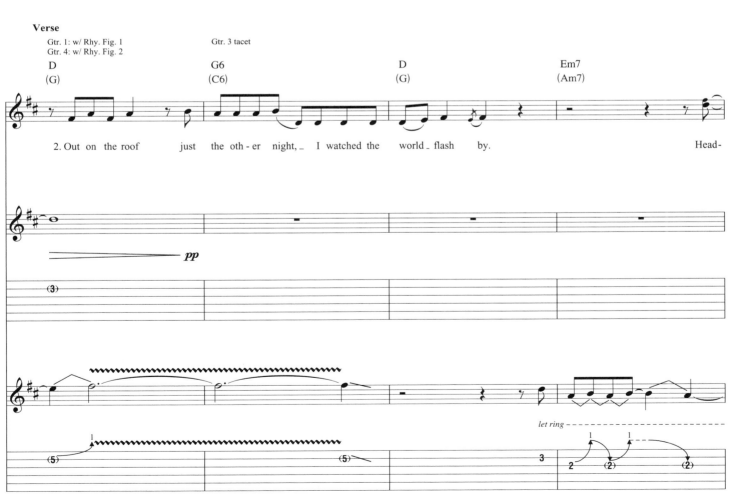

2. Out on the roof just the oth-er night,_ I watched the world _ flash by.

Head-

Gtr. 2: w/ Rhy. Fig. 5
1st time, Gtr. 3: w/ Riff C
2nd time, Gtr. 3: w/ Riff C (1st 3 meas.)

2nd time, Gtr. 3: w/ Fill 1

by. ___ Yeah, it's all ___ we've been giv-en, so you bet-ter start liv-in' right now. ___ And days go ___

Interlude

To Coda ⊕

Gtrs. 2 & 3: w/ Riff D

by. ___ Oh, and, uh, hoo, hoo. ___ Yeah, the days _ go ___

Rhy. Fig. 6

Gtr. 1

End Rhy. Fig. 6

by. ___ Oh, and, uh, hoo, hoo. ___

*Gtrs. 2 & 3

*Composite arrangement

Gtr. 1

Fill 1
Gtr. 3

Bridge
Half-time feel

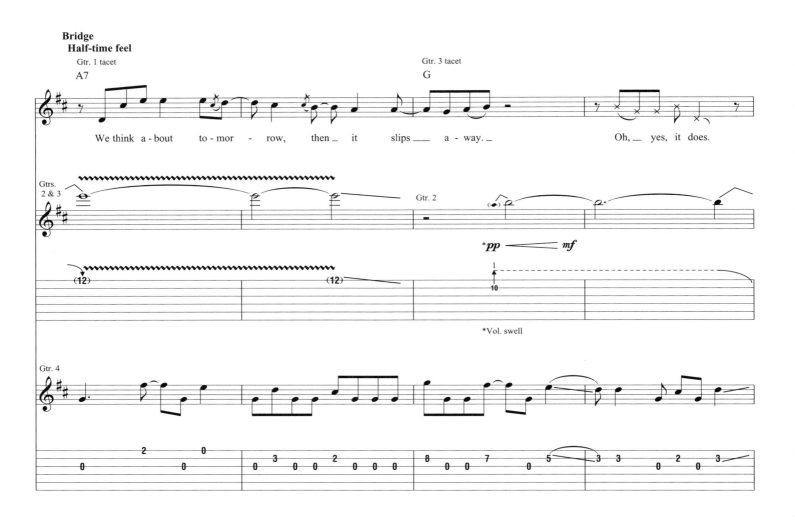

We think a-bout to-mor-row, then it slips a-way. Oh, yes, it does.

End half-time feel

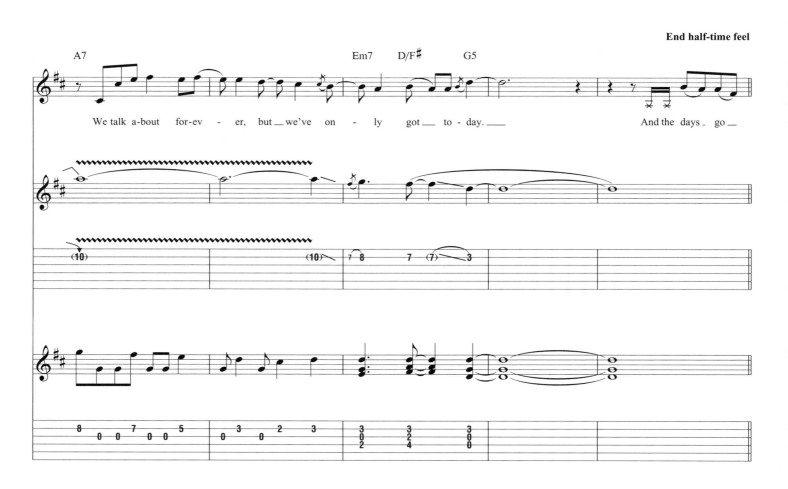

We talk a-bout for-ev - er, but we've on - ly got to-day. And the days go

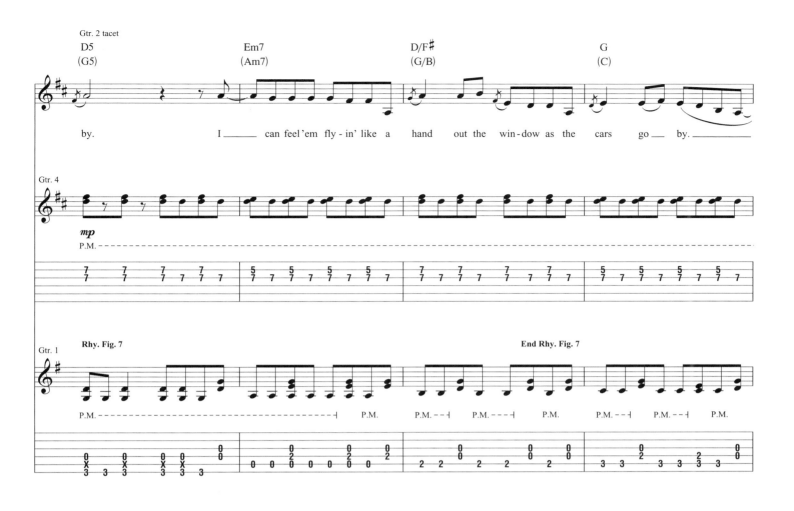

by. I ____ can feel 'em fly - in' like a hand out the win-dow as the cars go ___ by. ____

It's   all ____ we've been giv - en, so you bet - ter start liv - in', you

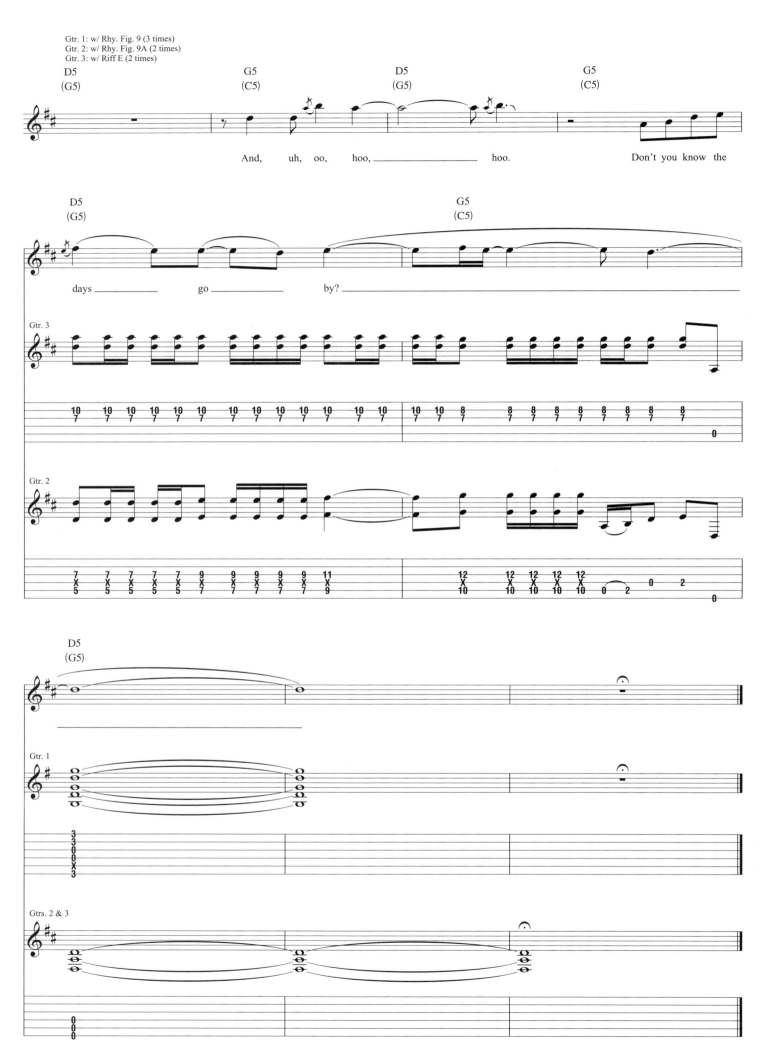

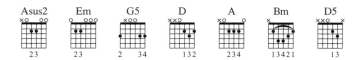

from *Act of Valor: The Album*

For You

Words and Music by Keith Urban and Monty Powell

Intro
Free time

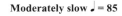

*Chord symbols reflect overall harmony.

Moderately slow ♩ = 85

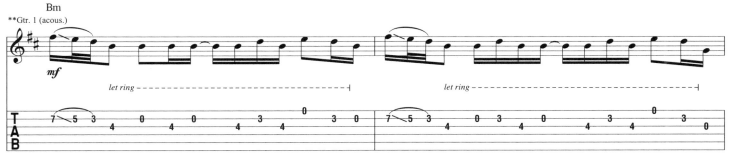

**Two gtrs. arr. for one.

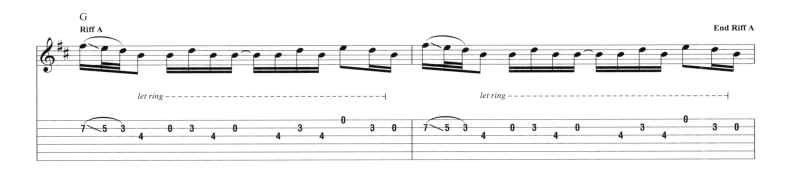

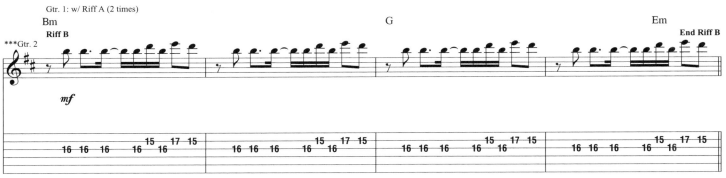

***Mandolin arr. for gtr.

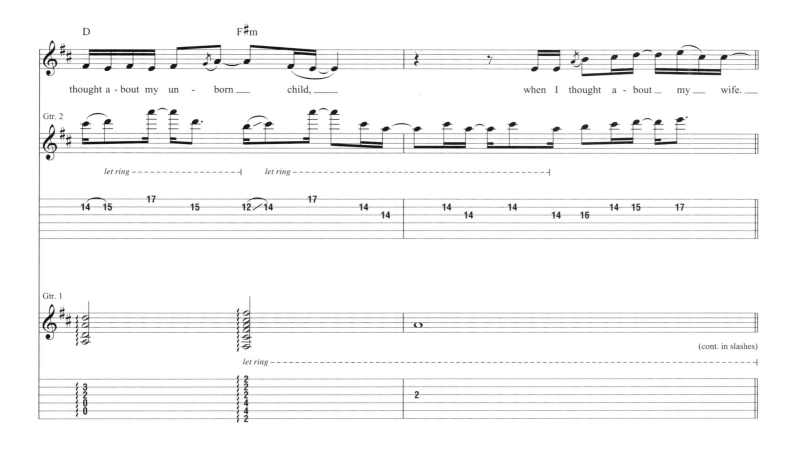

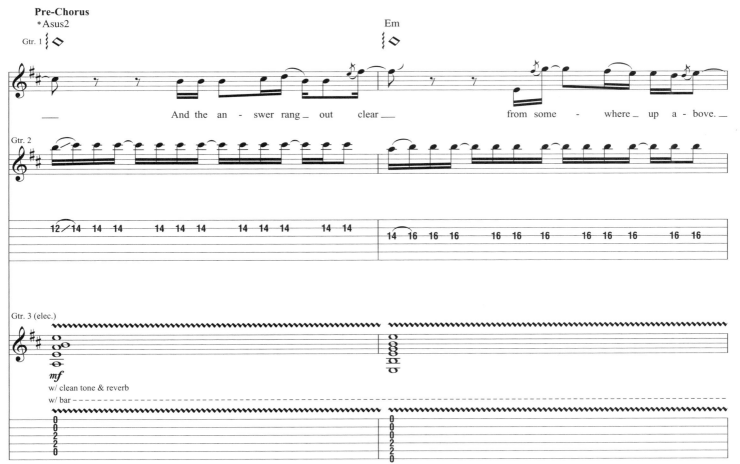

*See top of first page of song for chord diagrams pertaining to rhythm slashes.

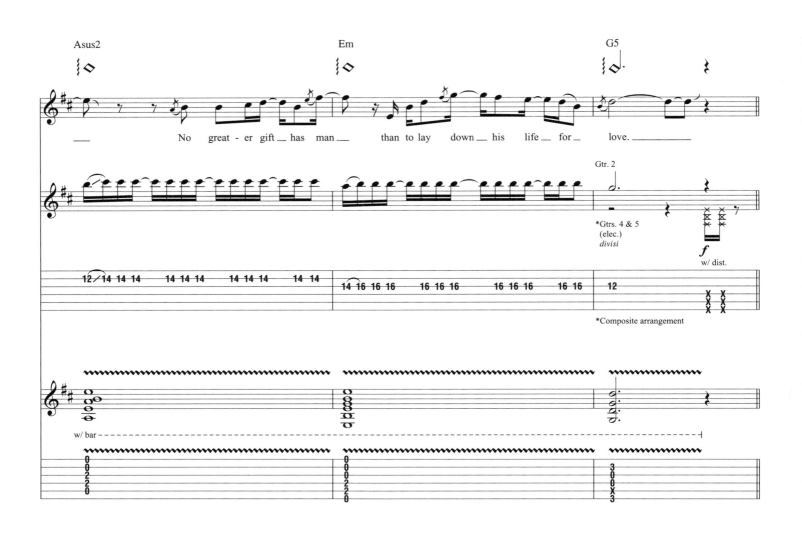

No great-er gift _ has man _ than to lay down _ his life _ for _ love. _____

Chorus

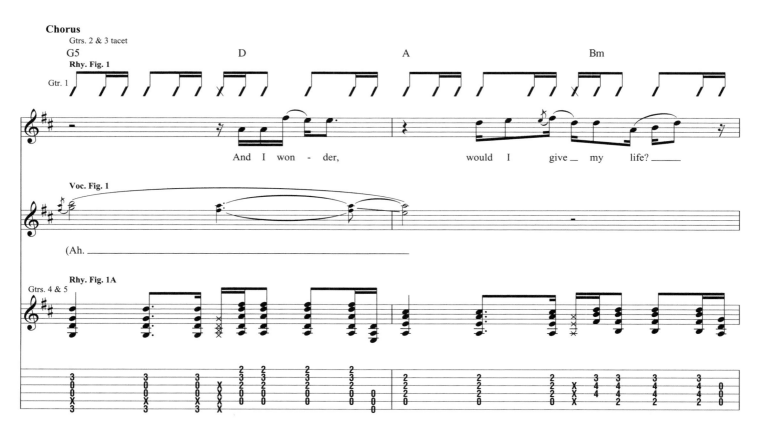

And I won - der, _____ would I give _ my life? _____

(Ah. _____

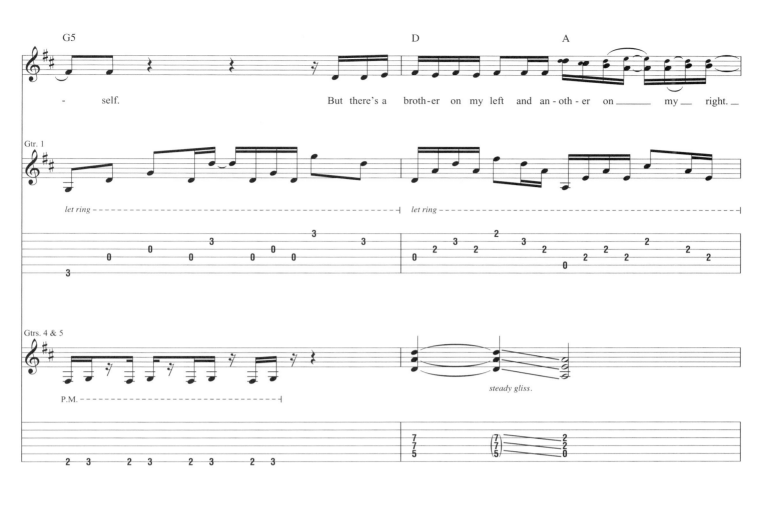

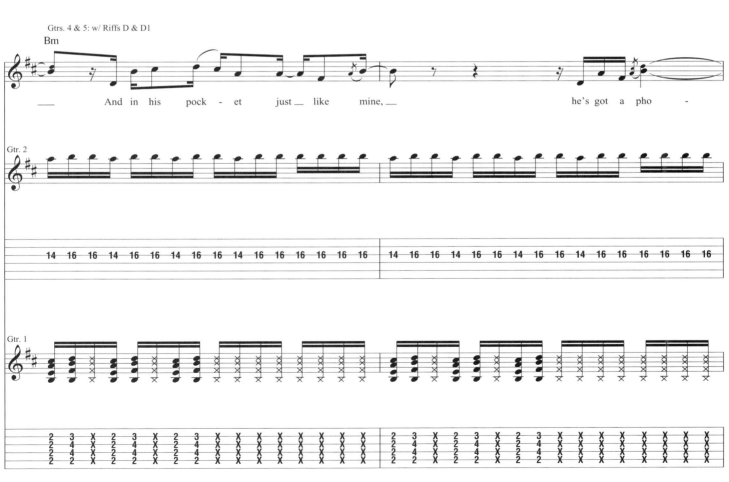

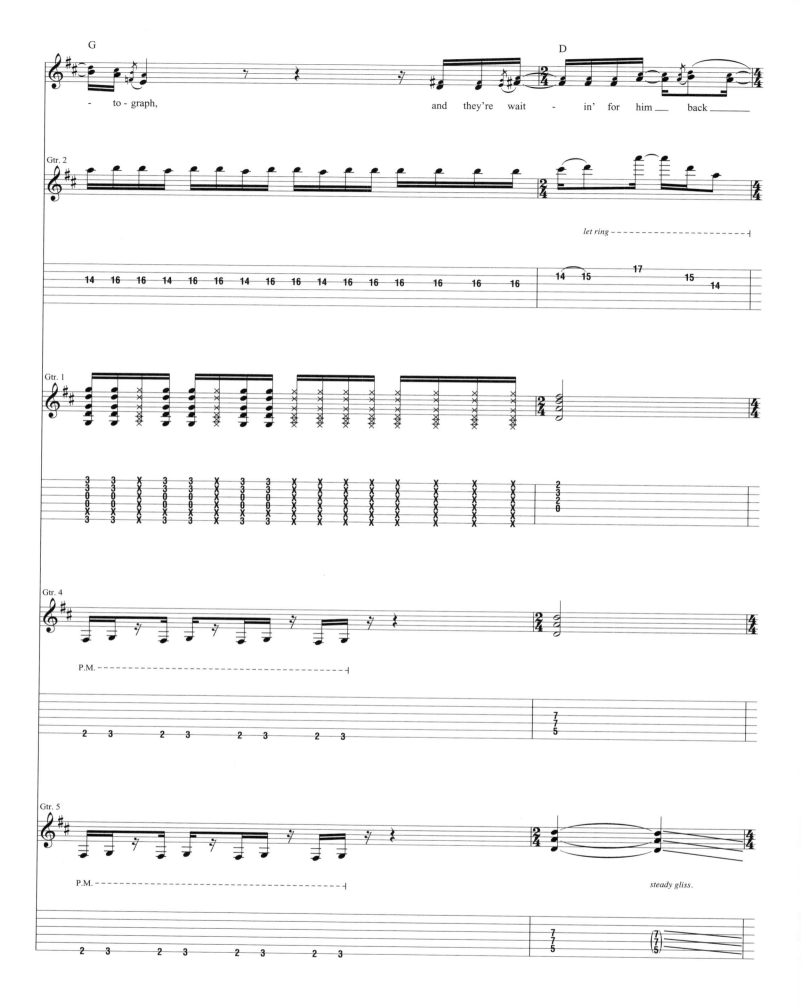

F#m

A

Gtr. 1

home. _____ And it's weigh-in' on ___ my ___ mind. ___ I'm not try-in' to be ___ a he -

Gtr. 2

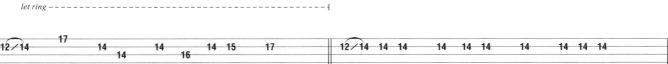

let ring -|

(cont. in slashes)

Gtr. 4

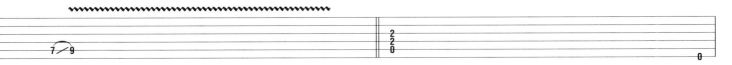

Gtr. 5

P.M. -

would, _____   yes I would. _____

let ring -

Bridge

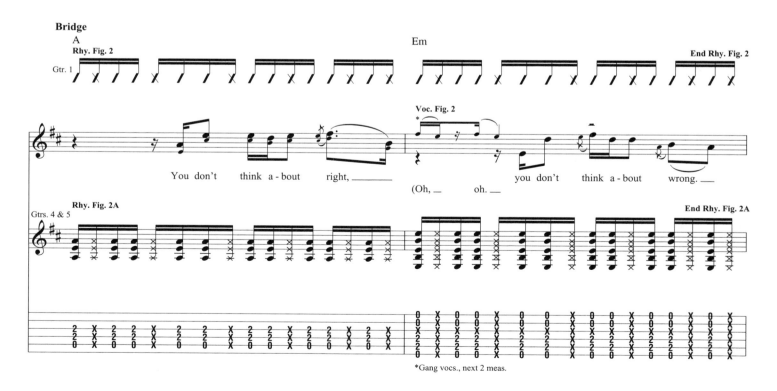

You don't   think a - bout   right, _____   you don't   think a - bout   wrong. _____
                                                        (Oh, ___   oh. ___

*Gang vocs., next 2 meas.

54

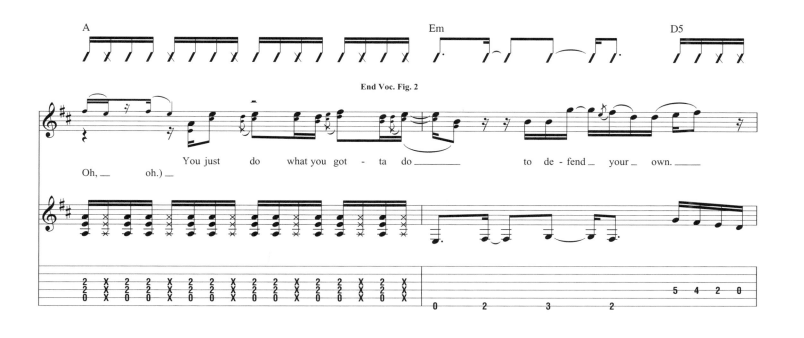

End Voc. Fig. 2

You just do what you got - ta do _____ to de - fend_ your_ own. _____

(Oh, _____ oh.) _____

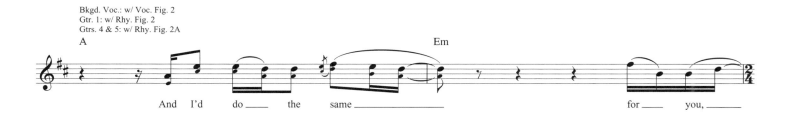

Bkgd. Voc.: w/ Voc. Fig. 2
Gtr. 1: w/ Rhy. Fig. 2
Gtrs. 4 & 5: w/ Rhy. Fig. 2A

And I'd do _____ the same _____ for _____ you, _____

Guitar Solo

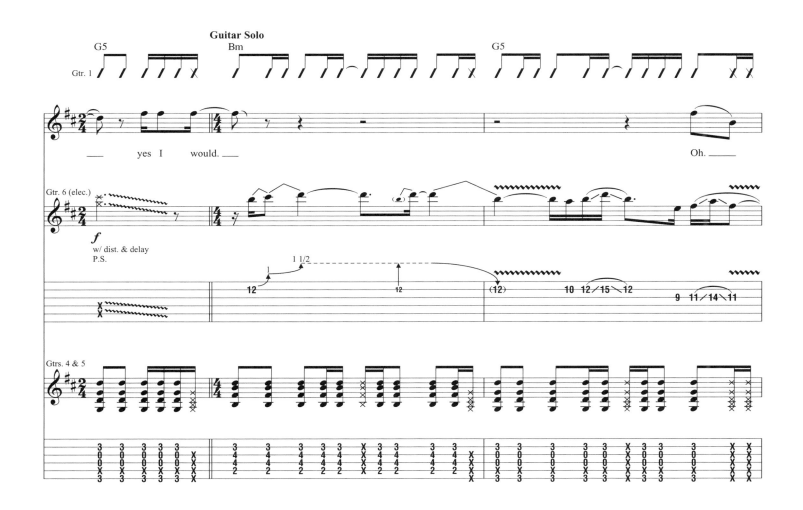

_____ yes I would. _____ Oh. _____

Gtr. 6 (elec.)
f
w/ dist. & delay
P.S.

Gtrs. 4 & 5

Yes   I   would. _____

Chorus
Bkgd. Voc.: w/ Voc. Fig. 1 (1st 2 meas.)
Gtrs. 4 & 5 tacet

And I would give __ my life. __

I would make that sac - ri - fice. _____

(Ah.) _____

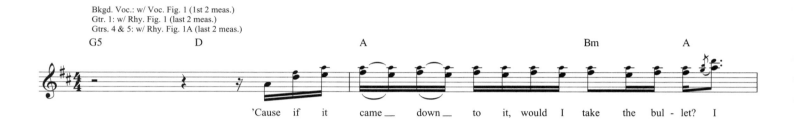

'Cause if it came down to it, would I take the bul - let? I

would, _____ yes, I would, _____ I'd do it for you. _____

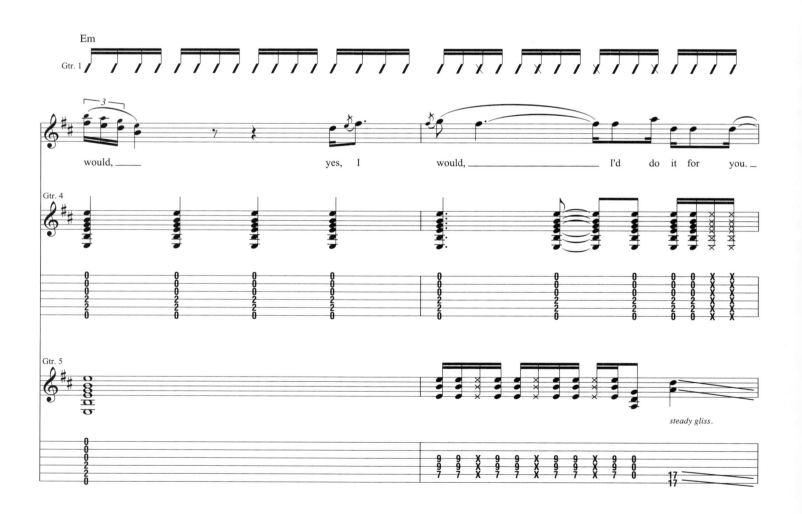

steady gliss.

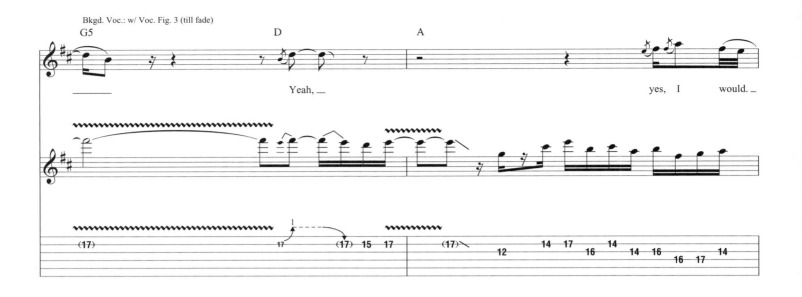

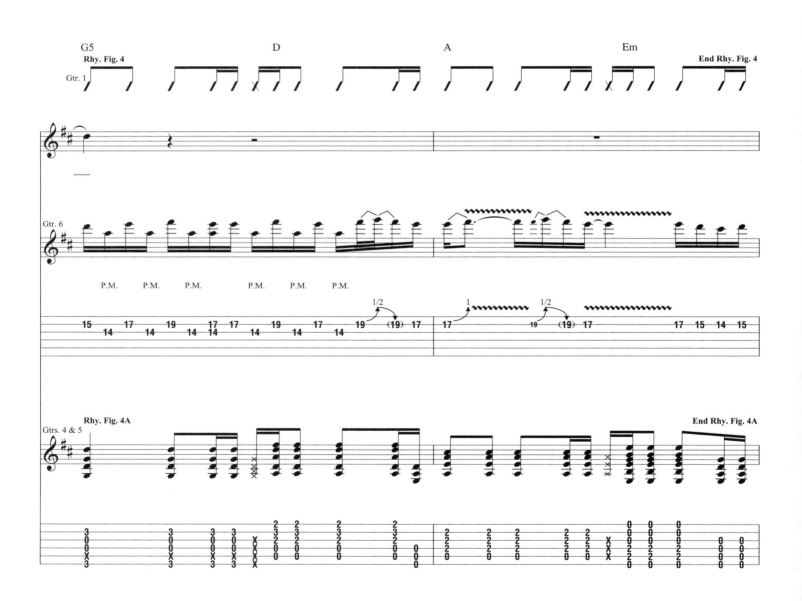

from *Defying Gravity*

Kiss a Girl

Words and Music by Monty Powell and Keith Urban

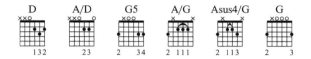

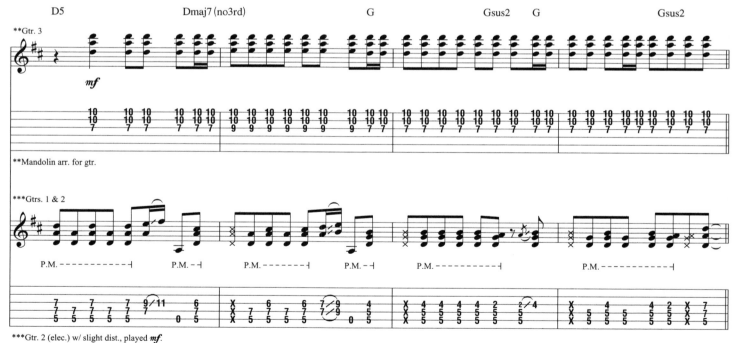

***Gtr. 2 (elec.) w/ slight dist., played *mf*.
    Composite arrangement

Verse

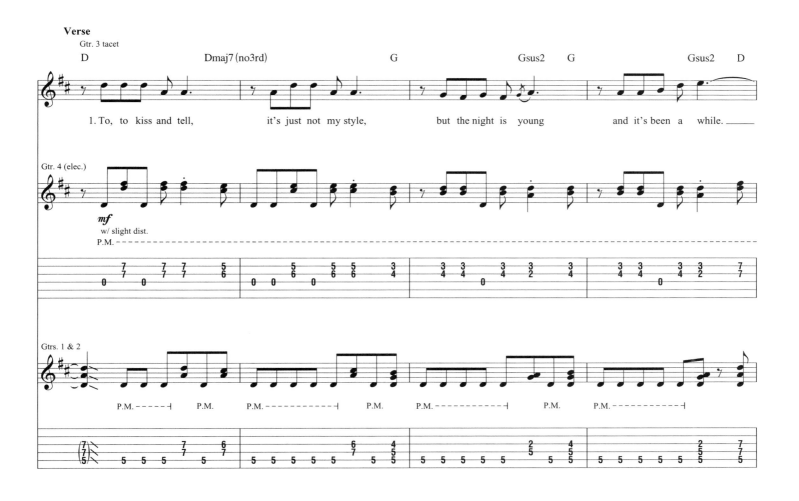

1. To, to kiss and tell, it's just not my style, but the night is young and it's been a while. _____

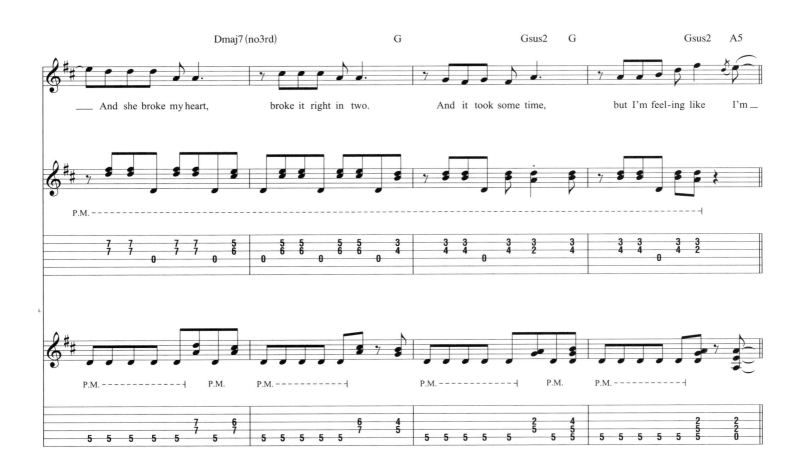

_____ And she broke my heart, broke it right in two. And it took some time, but I'm feel-ing like I'm _____

Don't wan-na go too far,____ just to take it slow.____ But I should-n't be ____ lone-

-ly in this big old world._____ I _____ wan - na kiss a girl.____

End Rhy. Fig. 1

End Riff A

Interlude

Gtr. 5 tacet

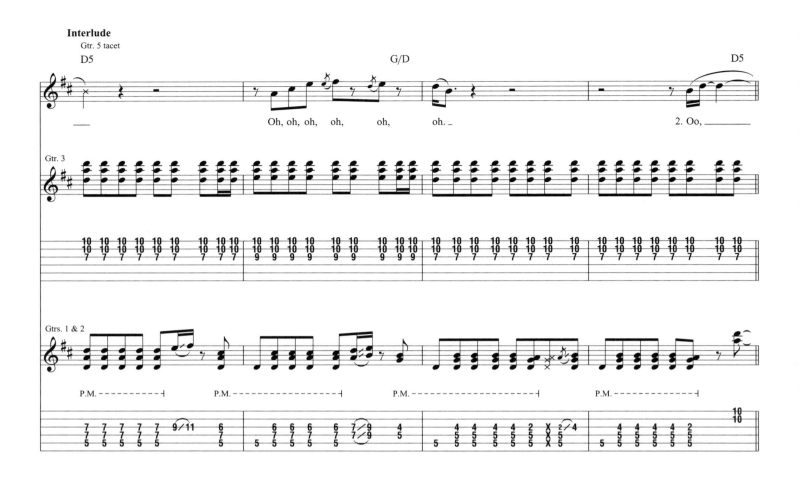

Oh, oh, oh, oh, oh, oh.

2. Oo, _____

Verse

___ it's that mo-ment when you start clos-ing in. First you're hold-ing back, then sur-ren-der-ing. _____

*See top of first page of song for chord diagrams pertaining to rhythm slashes.

It can start a fire, and light up the sky. Such a sim-ple thing, do you wan-na try? _____

Pre-Chorus

_____ Are you read-y to _____ say good-bye _____ to all _____ these blues. _____

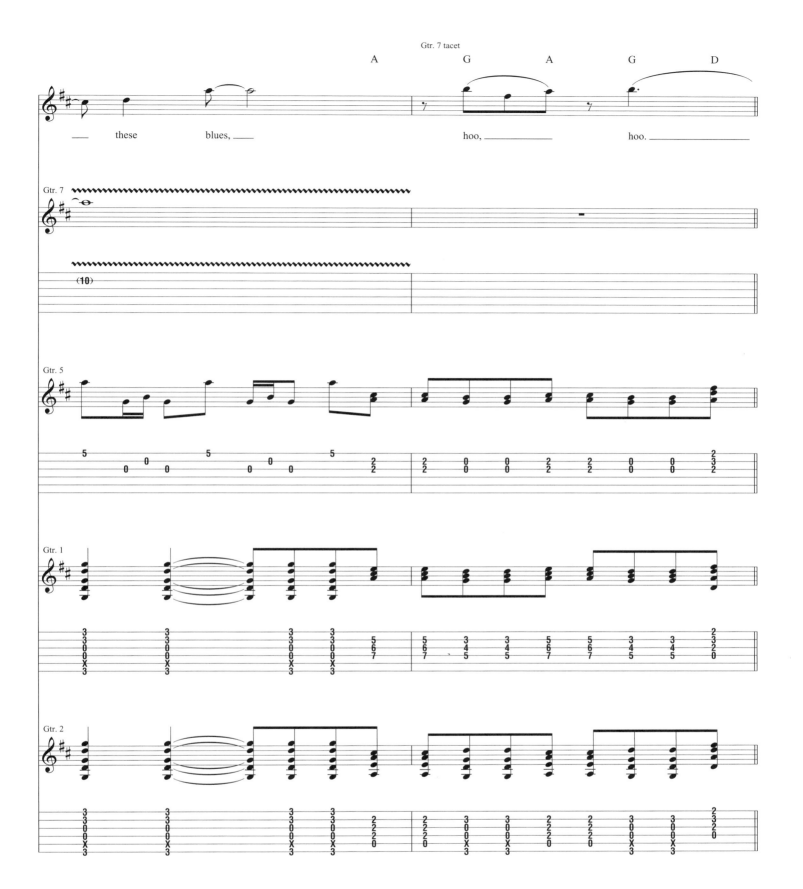

75

Chorus

I wan-na kiss a girl, I wan-na hold her tight. May-be make a lit-tle mag-ic, ba - by.

let ring

let ring

*Gtrs. 1 & 2

*Composite arrangement

Gtrs. 8 & 9 tacet

I don't wan - na go too far, _____ just to take it slow. _____ But don't wan - na be lone-

Outro

Gtr. 5 tacet

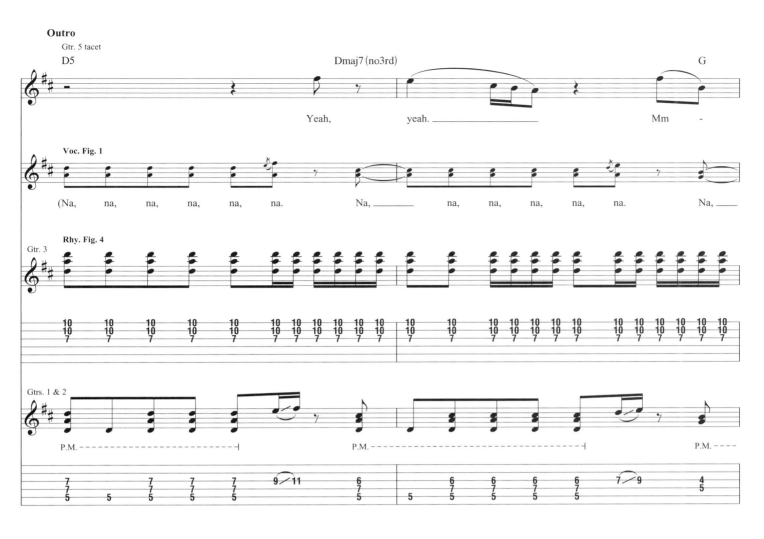

Yeah, yeah. Mm-

(Na, na, na, na, na, na. Na, na, na, na, na, na. Na,

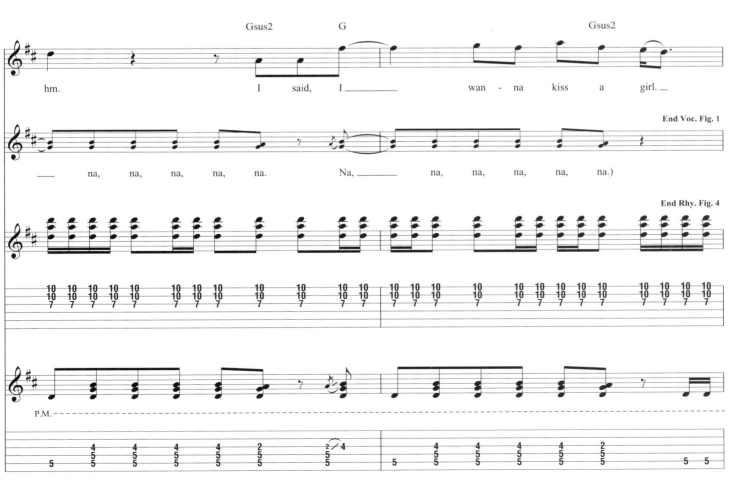

hm. I said, I wan-na kiss a girl.

na, na, na, na, na. Na, na, na, na, na, na.)

End Voc. Fig. 1

End Rhy. Fig. 4

from *Get Closer*

Long Hot Summer

Words and Music by Keith Urban and Richard Marx

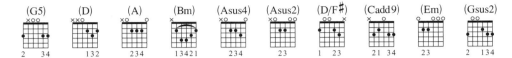

Gtrs. 1 - 6, 10 & 11: Capo I

*Symbols in parentheses represent chord names respective to capoed guitar. Symbols above represent actual sounding chords. Capoed fret is "0" in tab. Chord symbols reflect overall harmony.

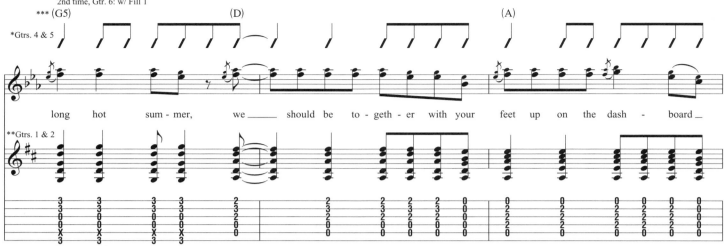

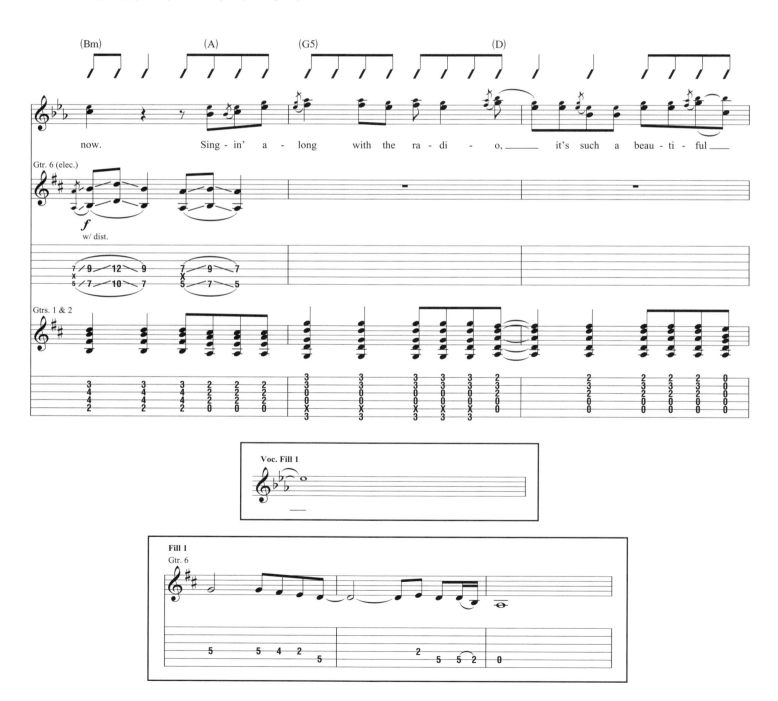

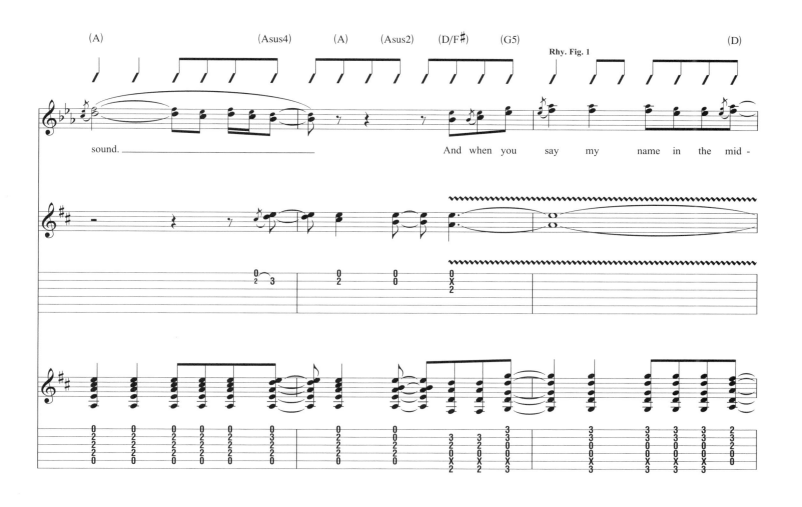

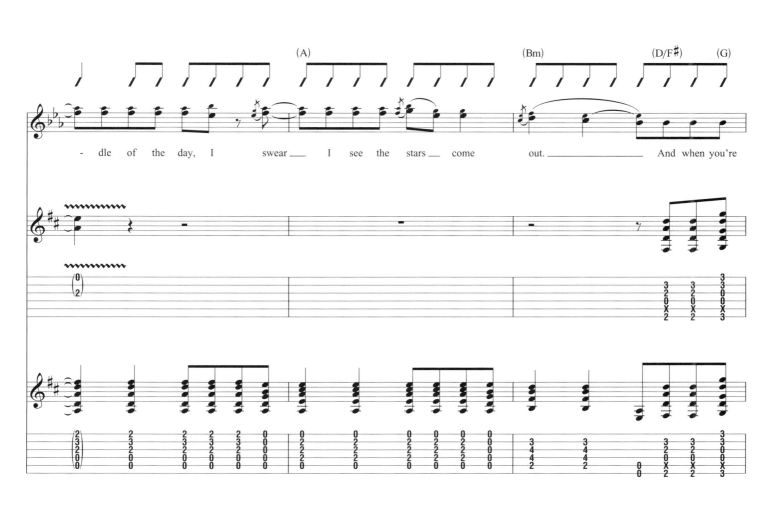

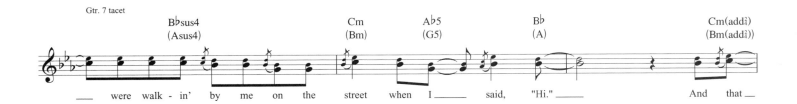

Gtr. 7 tacet

were walk - in' by me on the street when I ___ said, "Hi." ___ And that ___

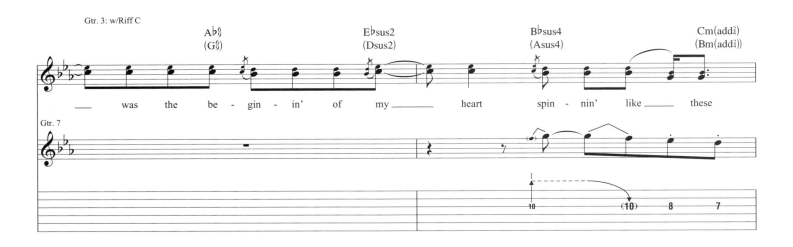

Gtr. 3: w/Riff C

was the be - gin - in' of my ___ heart spin - nin' like ___ these

Gtr. 7

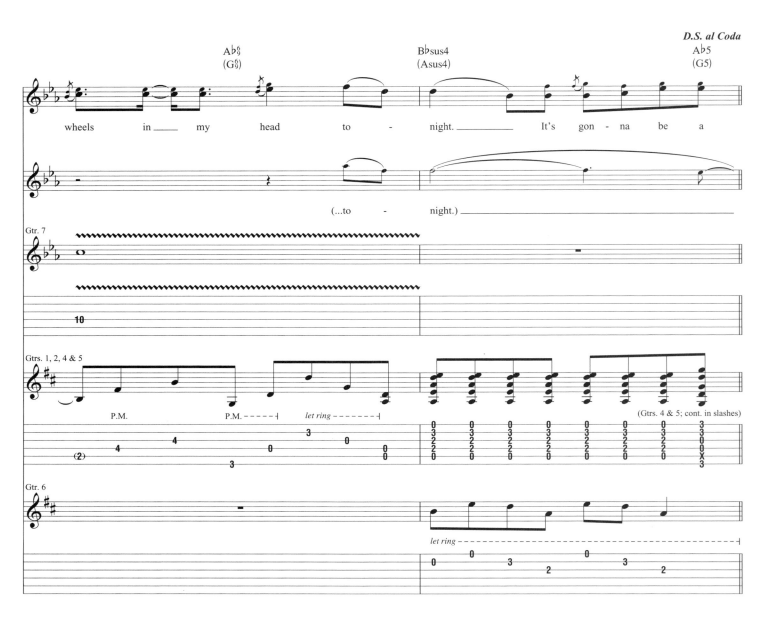

D.S. al Coda

wheels in ___ my head to - night. ___ It's gon - na be a

(...to - night.) ___

Gtr. 7

Gtrs. 1, 2, 4 & 5

P.M.   P.M.‑ ‑ ‑ ‑ | *let ring* ‑ ‑ ‑ ‑ ‑ | (Gtrs. 4 & 5; cont. in slashes)

Gtr. 6

let ring ‑ ‑ ‑ ‑ ‑ ‑ ‑ ‑ ‑ ‑ ‑ ‑ ‑ ‑ ‑ ‑ |

Bridge

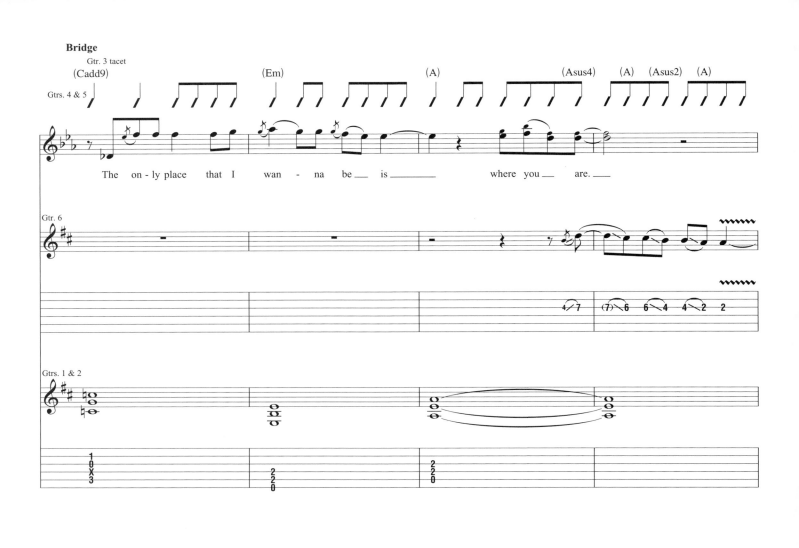

The on-ly place that I wan-na be ___ is ___ where you ___ are. ___

'Cause an-y more than a heart-beat a-way ___ is just too ___ far. ___

(cont. in slashes)

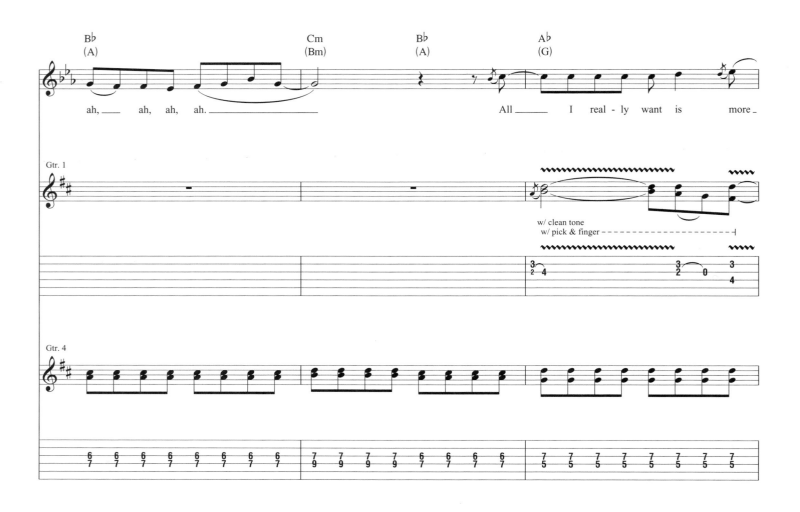

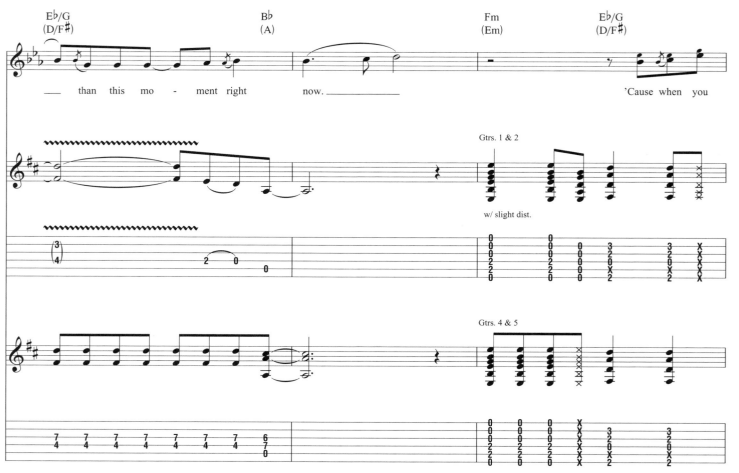

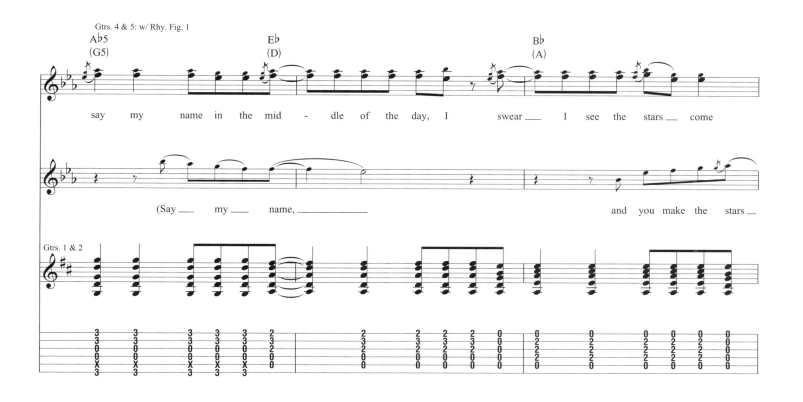

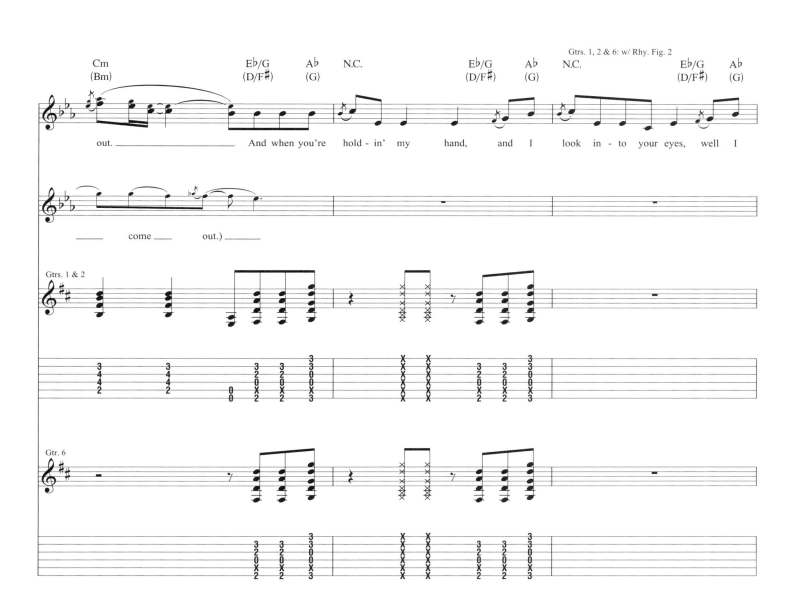

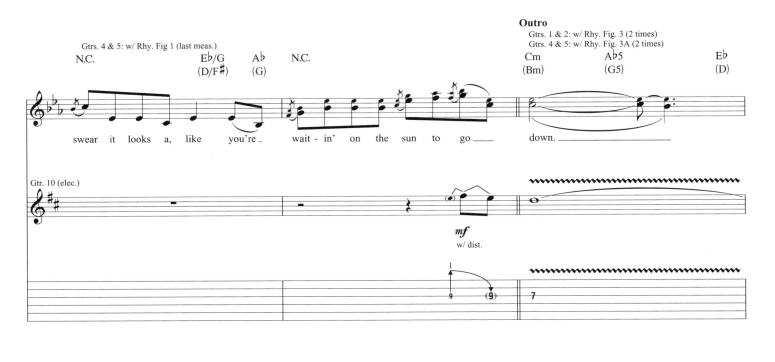

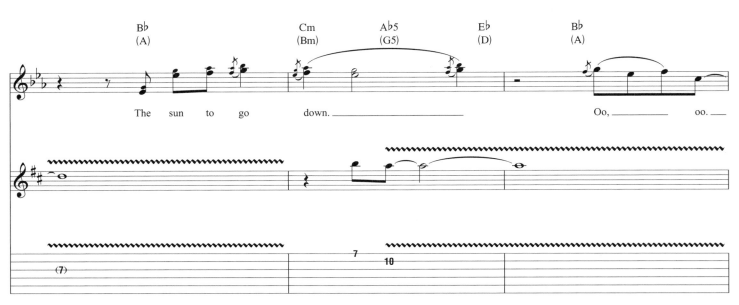

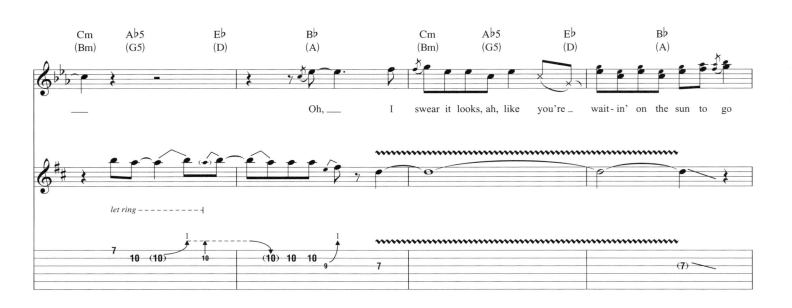

down. _____ Oh, _____ whoa. _____

from *Be Here*

Making Memories of Us

Words and Music by Rodney Crowell

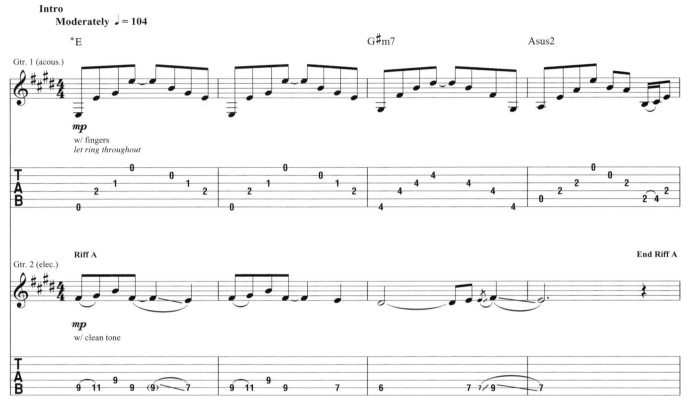

*Chord symbols reflect implied harmony.

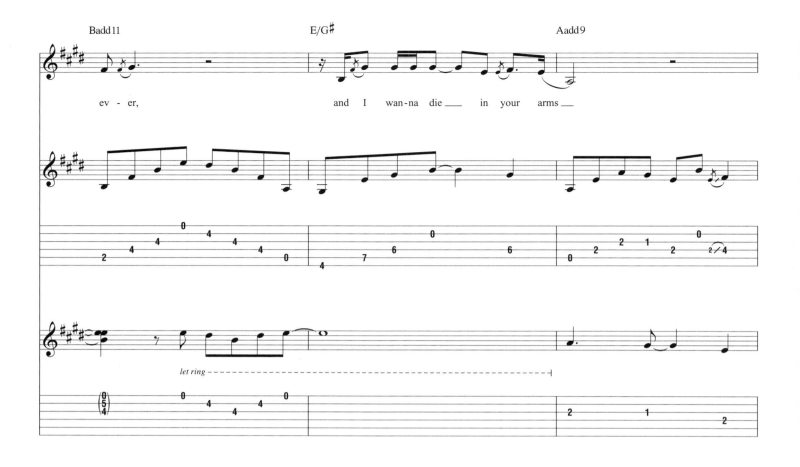

ev - er,

and I wan-na die____ in your arms____

in a cab-in by a mead-ow where the wild_____ bees____ swarm._____

End Riff B

Chorus

And I'm gon-na love ___ you ___ like no-bod-y loves you. ___

And I'll earn ___ your trust, mak-in' mem-'ries of ___ us.

Verse

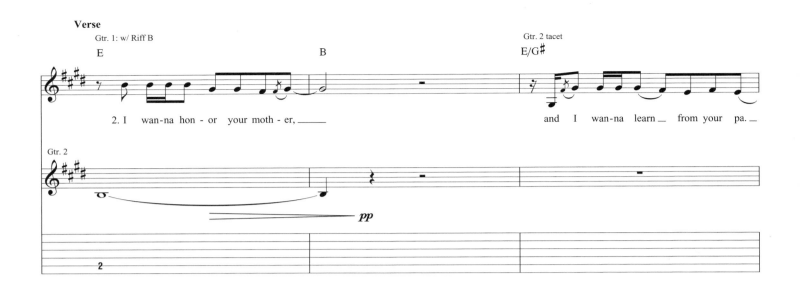

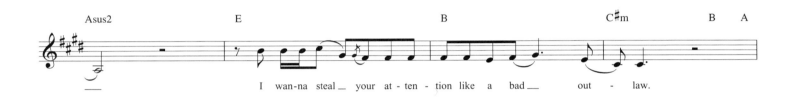

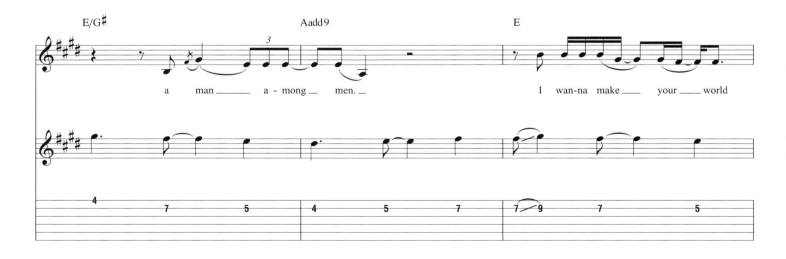

We'll fol-low the rain - bow ___ wher - ev - er the four ___ winds blow. ___

And there'll be a new ___ day ___ com - in' your ___

Verse

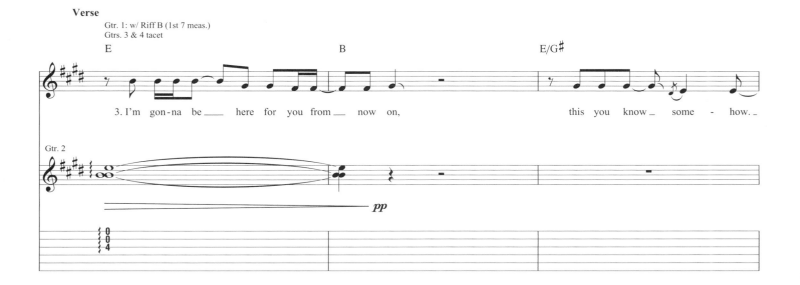

3. I'm gon-na be ___ here for you from ___ now on,   this you know ___ some - how. ___

You've been stretched _ to the lim - its, but it's all _____ right _

*Vol. swell

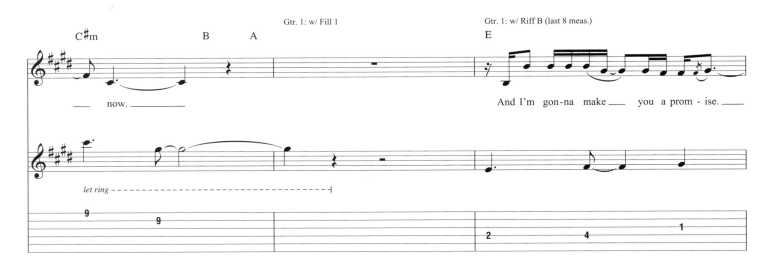

Gtr. 1: w/ Fill 1

Gtr. 1: w/ Riff B (last 8 meas.)

_ now. _____

And I'm gon-na make ___ you a prom - ise. ___

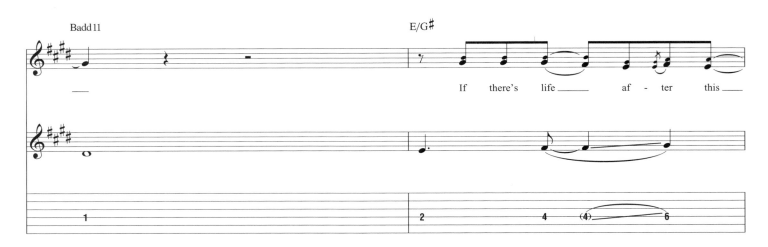

If there's life ___ af - ter this ___

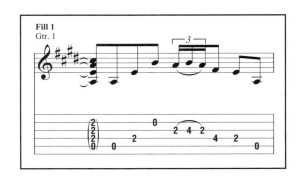

Fill 1
Gtr. 1

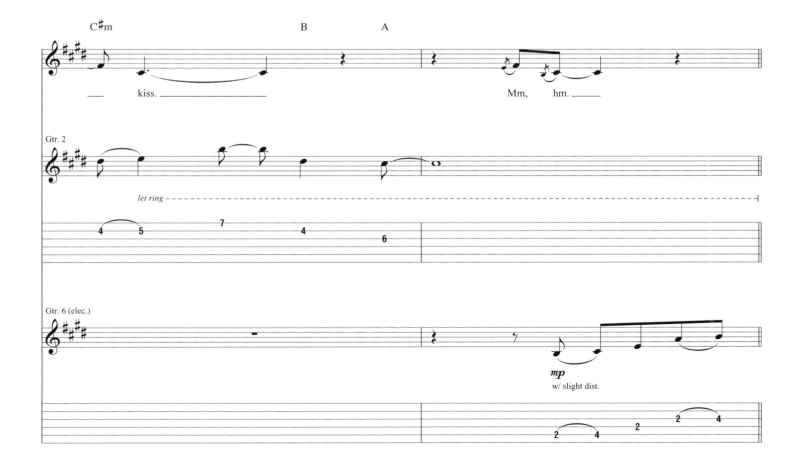

Gtr. 1: w/ Rhy. Fig. 1

And I'm gon - na love ___ you ___ like no - bod - y loves you. ___

Gtr. 1: w/ Rhy. Fig. 2

And I'll earn _ your trust, mak - in' mem-'ries of _____ us. Whoa, ___

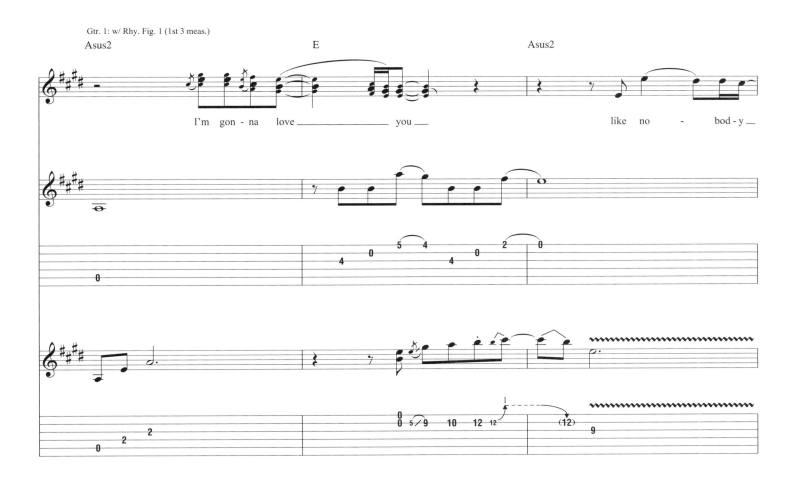

Outro

from *Get Closer*

Put You in a Song

Words and Music by Keith Urban, Sarah Buxton and Jedd Hughes

Drop D tuning:
(low to high) D-A-D-G-B-E

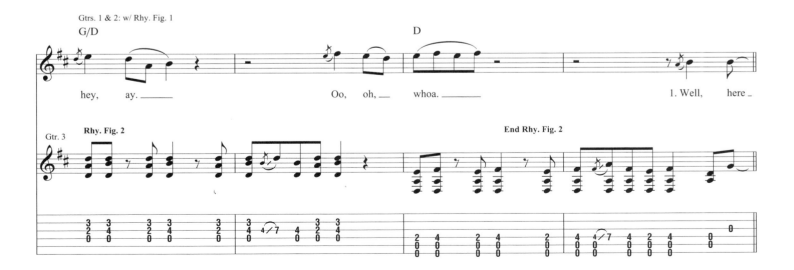

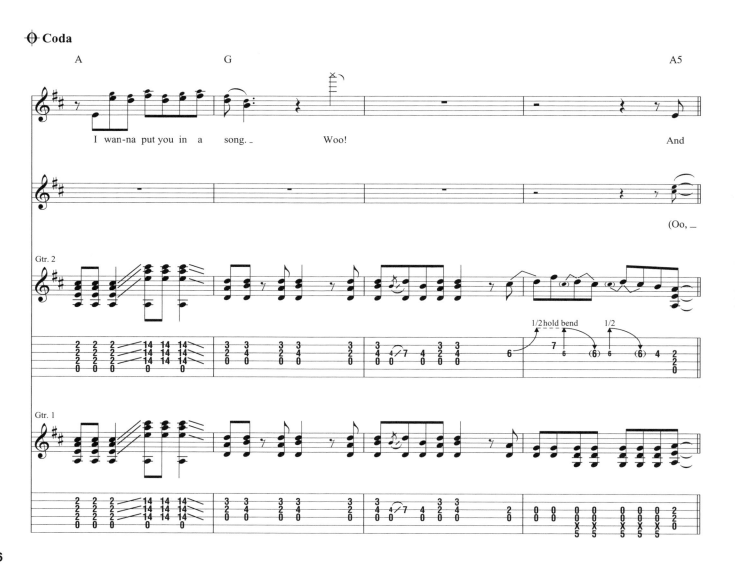

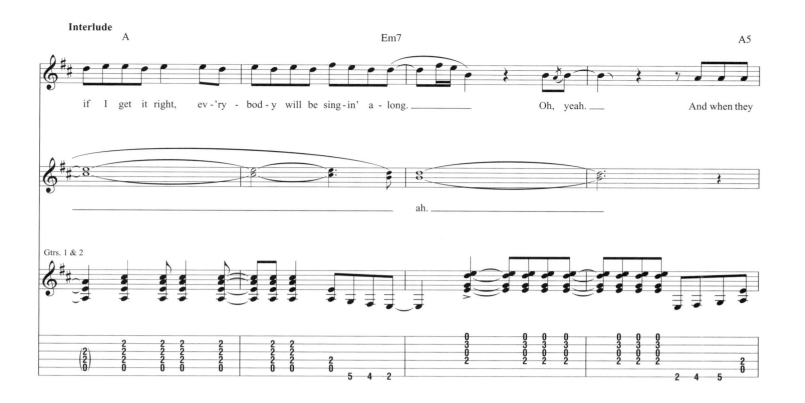

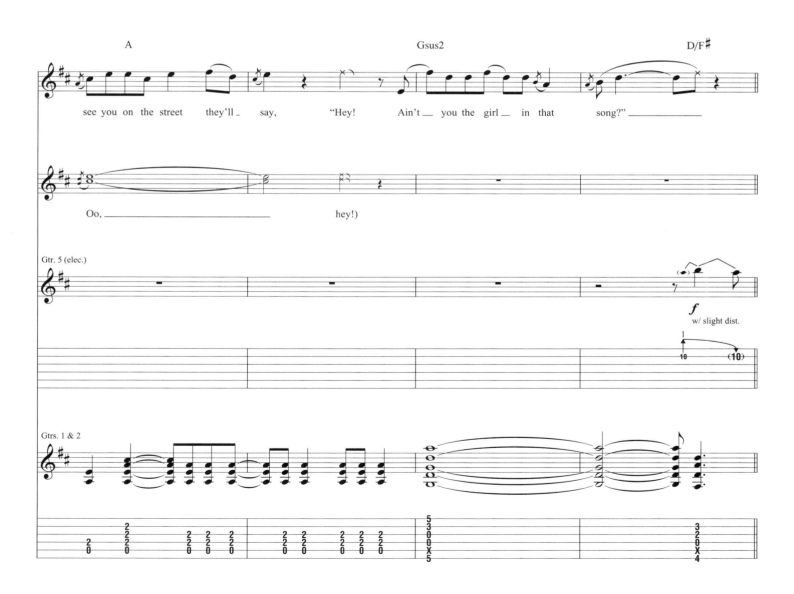

Guitar Solo

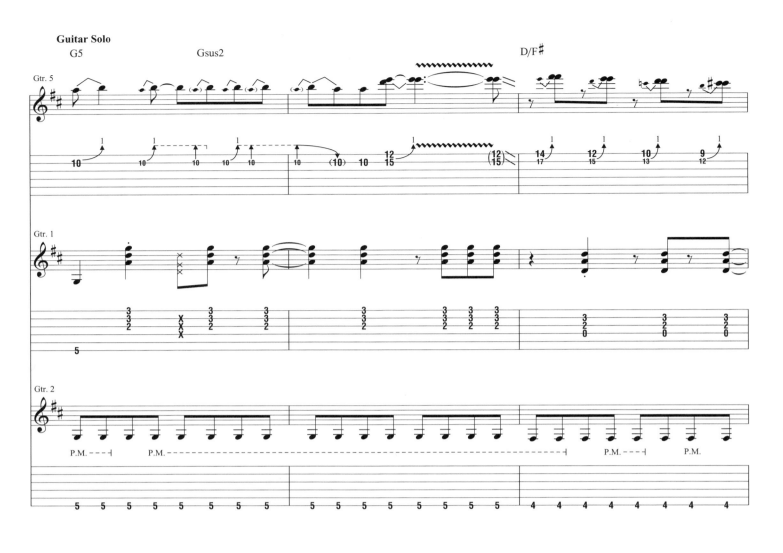

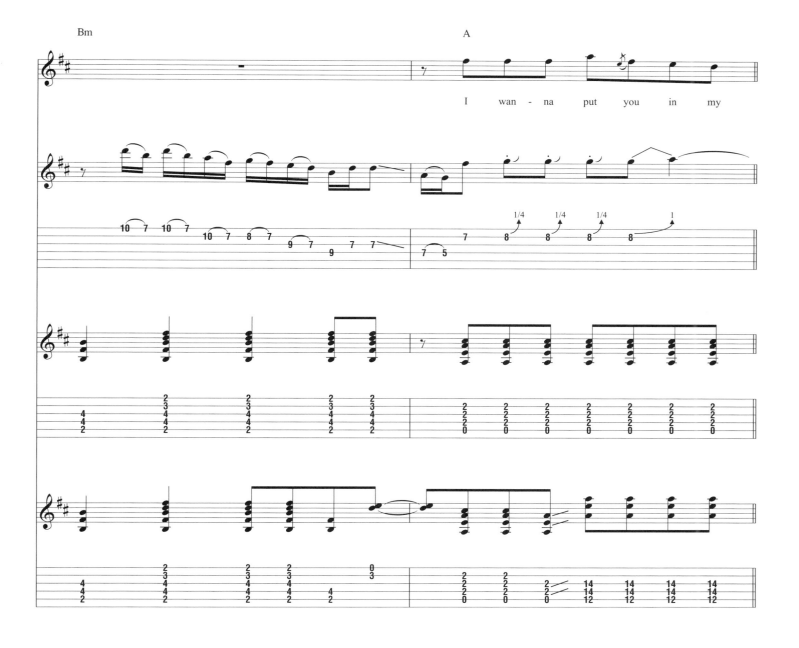

Bm

A

I wan - na put you in my

Chorus

Gtrs. 1 & 2: w/ Rhy. Fig. 3

G5

D5

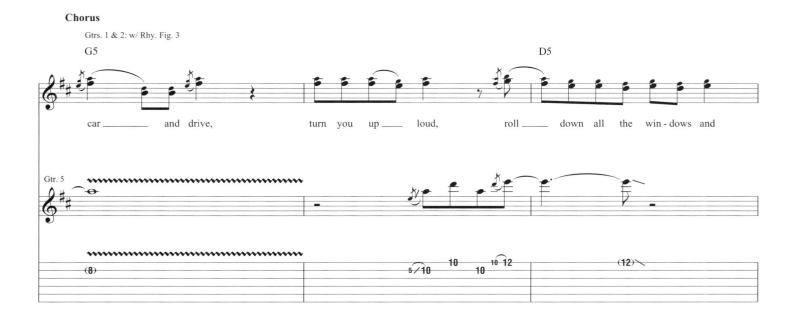

car _____ and drive,   turn you up ___ loud,   roll ____ down all the win - dows and

Gtr. 5

120

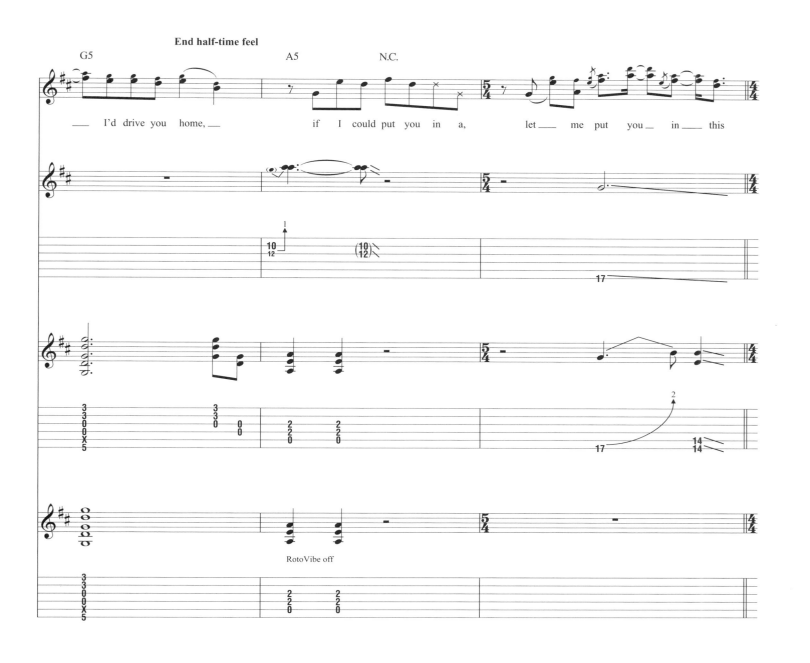

End half-time feel

G5   A5   N.C.

I'd drive you home,   if I could put you in a,   let   me put   you   in   this

RotoVibe off

Interlude

Gtrs. 1 & 2: w/ Rhy. Fig. 1 (2 times)

G/D   D

song.   Ay,   ay,   eah.

Gtr. 5

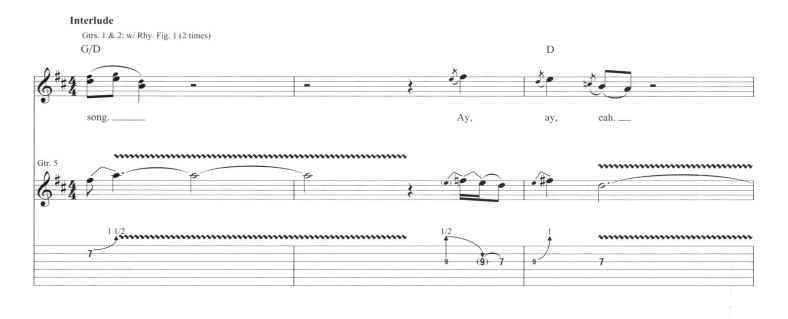

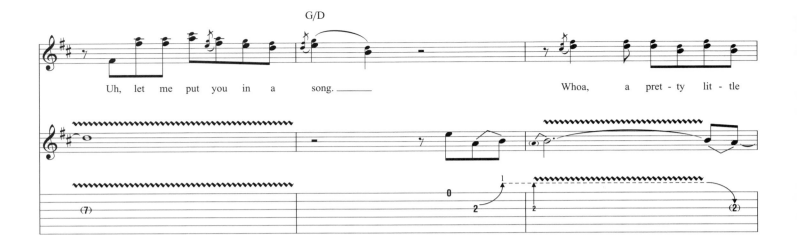

Uh, let me put you in a song. _____ Whoa, a pret - ty lit - tle

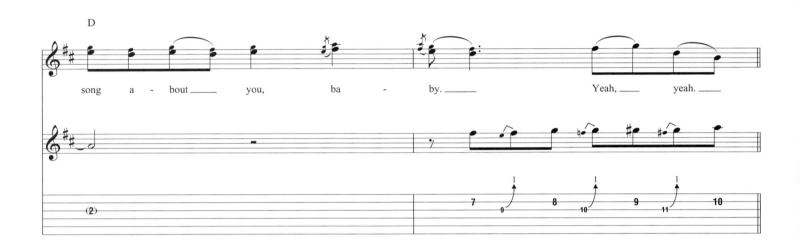

song a - bout _____ you, ba - by. _____ Yeah, _____ yeah. _____

Outro-Guitar Solo

Gtr. 2: w/ Rhy. Fig. 1 (1 1/2 times)

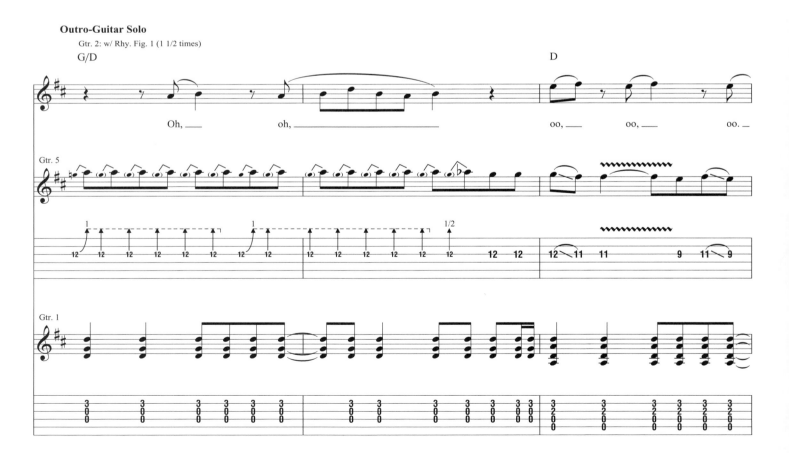

Oh, _____ oh, _____ oo, _____ oo, _____ oo. _____

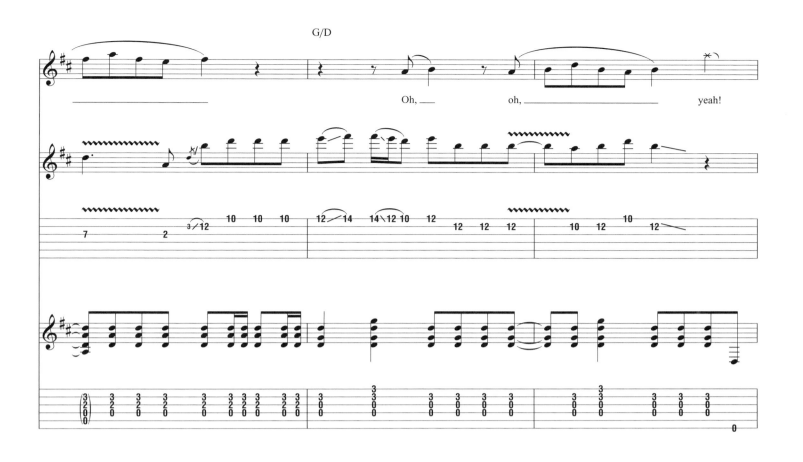

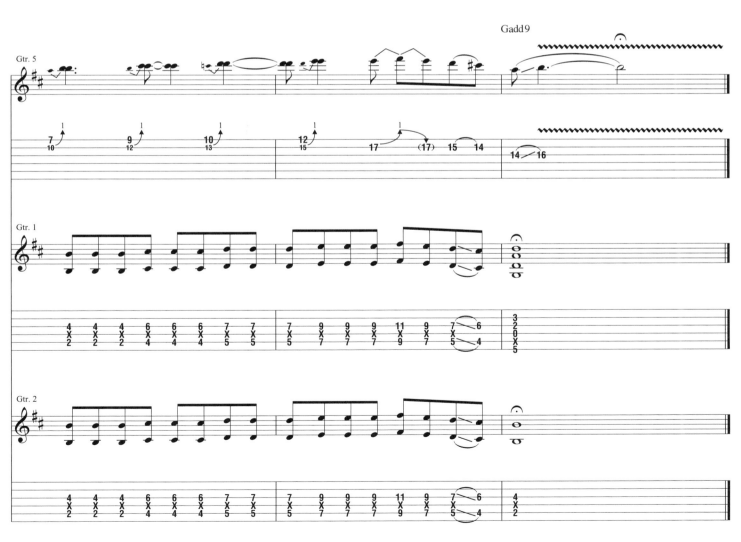

Roller Coaster

Words and Music by Keith Urban and Matthew Rollings

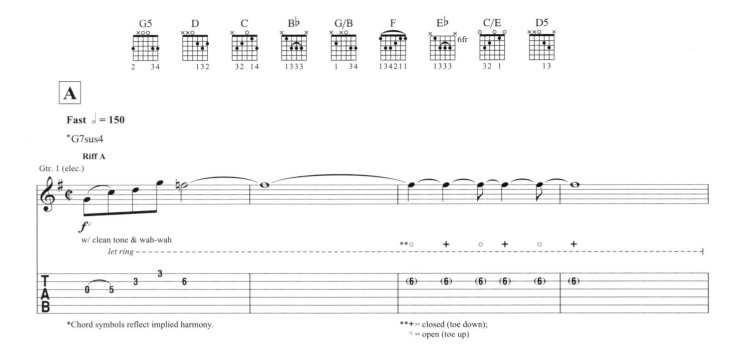

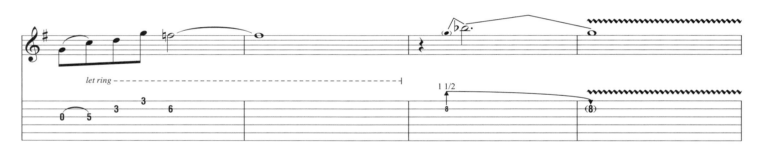

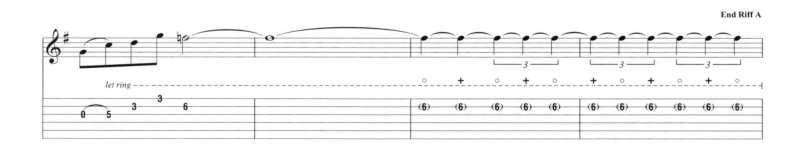

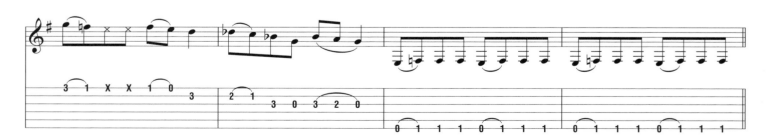

B

*See top of first page of song for chord diagrams pertaining to rhythm slashes.

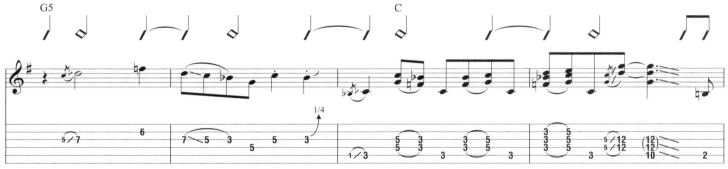

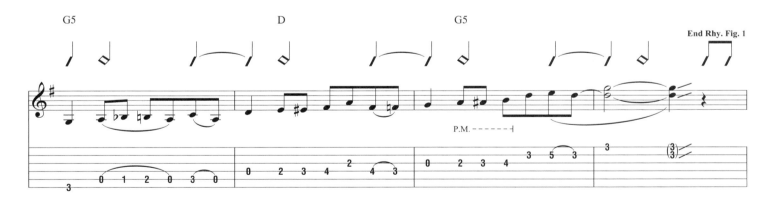

Gtr. 2: w/ Rhy. Fig. 1

G5

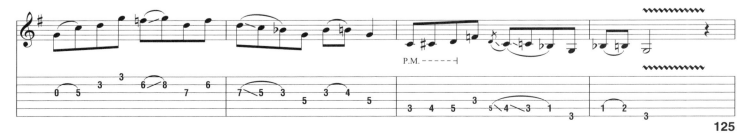

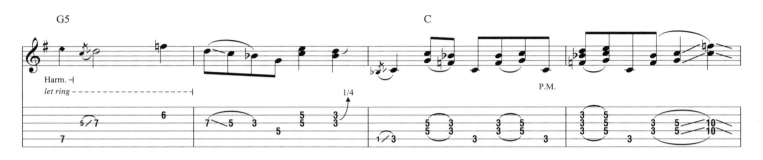

C

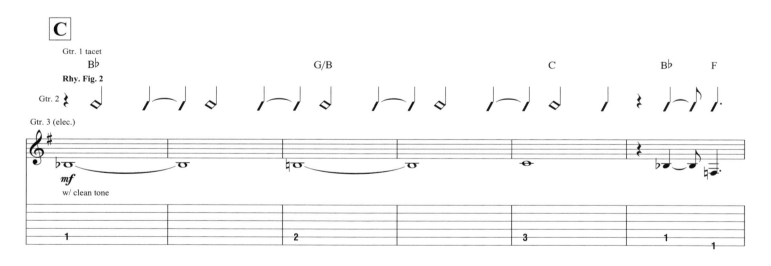

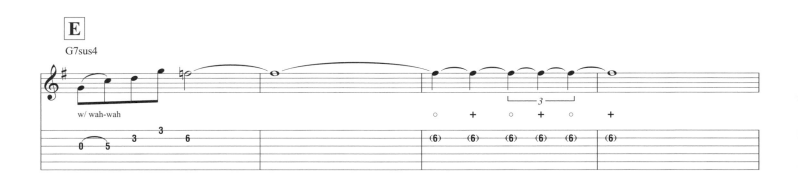

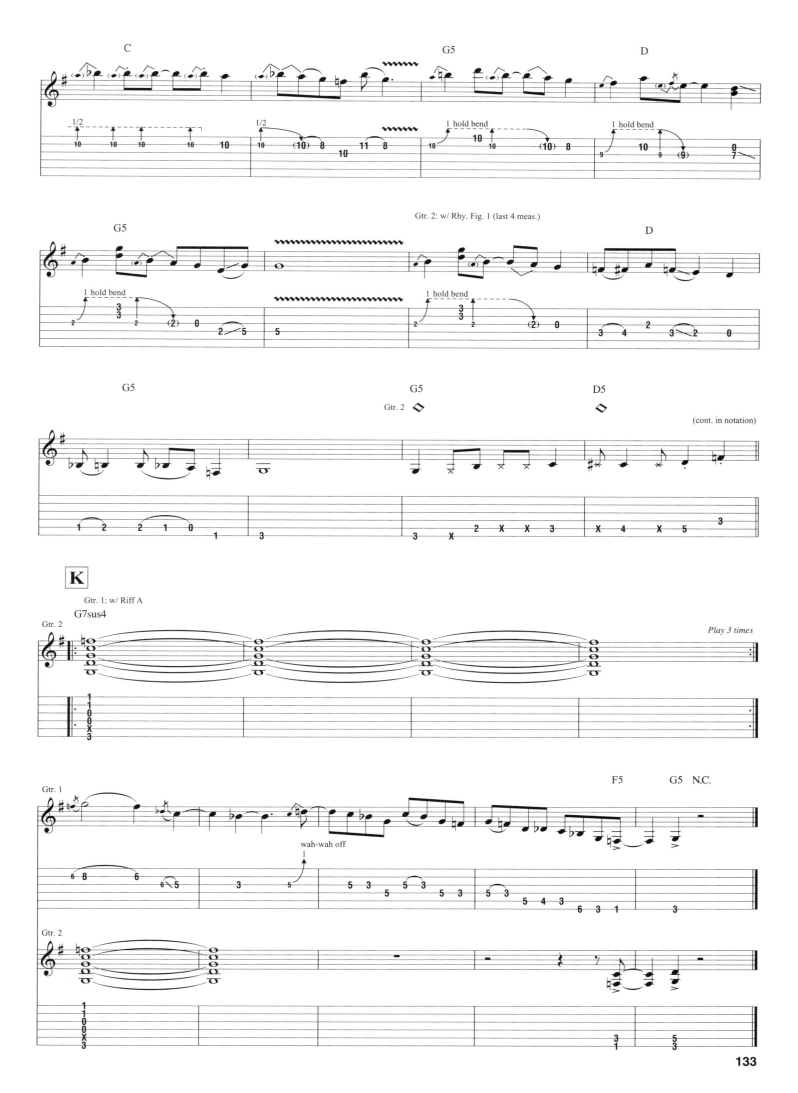

from *Days Go By*

Somebody Like You

Words and Music by John Shanks and Keith Urban

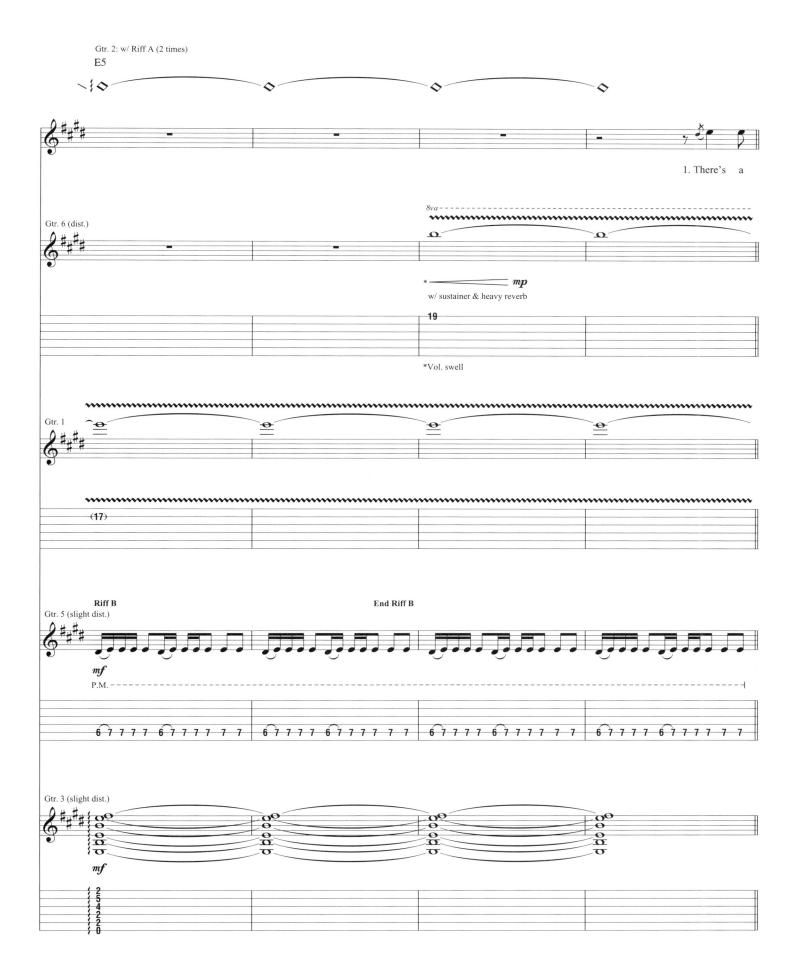

1. There's   a

Verse

Gtr. 4 tacet
Gtr. 6 tacet
Gtr. 5: w/ Riff B (4 times)
*E5

new wind _ blow-ing like I've nev - er known. _ I'm breath - ing _ deep-er than I've ev - er done. _ And it

Gtr. 1

Gtr. 5

Gtr. 2

Gtr. 3

*Chord symbols reflect overall harmony.

Gtr. 3 tacet
A5
E5
sure feels good to fi-n'lly feel the way I do.
Now, I wan-na
Gtr. 7 (dist.)
*mp
w/ heavy reverb
*Vol. swells
Gtr. 1
Gtr. 2
Harm.
Gtrs. 2 & 7 tacet
B5
A5
Gtr. 2: w/ Riff A
E5
love some-bod-y, love some-bod-y like you.
2. And I'm let-ting
Gtr. 1
Riff C
Gtr. 5
End Riff C
P.M.

Verse

Gtr. 1 tacet
Gtr. 5: w/ Riff B (1 1/2 times)

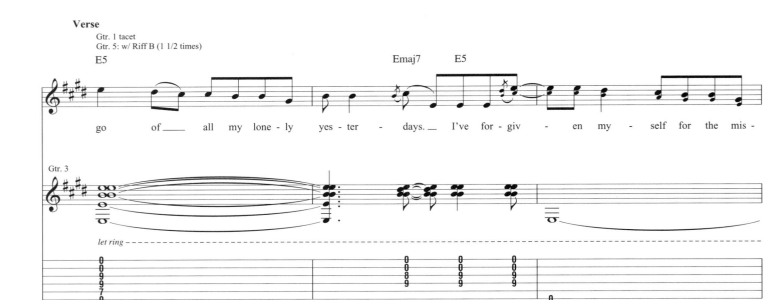

go of _____ all my lone - ly yes - ter - days. I've for - giv - en my - self for the mis-

takes I've made. _ Now there's just one thing, _ the on - ly thing I wan - na do. _

Gtr. 2: w/ Riff A
Gtr. 4 tacet
E
Bsus4
Mm, hmm. I wan-na love some-bod-y, love
Gtr. 5
P.M.
Gtr. 3
Asus2
Gtr. 2: w/ Riff A
E5
some-bod-y like you.
Yeah, I wan-na feel the
Gtr. 4
Gtr. 5
Gtr. 3

Chorus

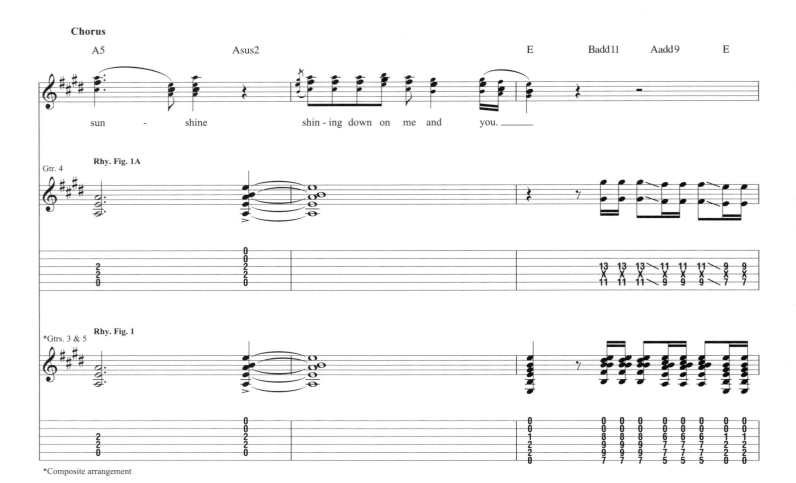

sun - shine shin-ing down on me and you. ___

*Composite arrangement

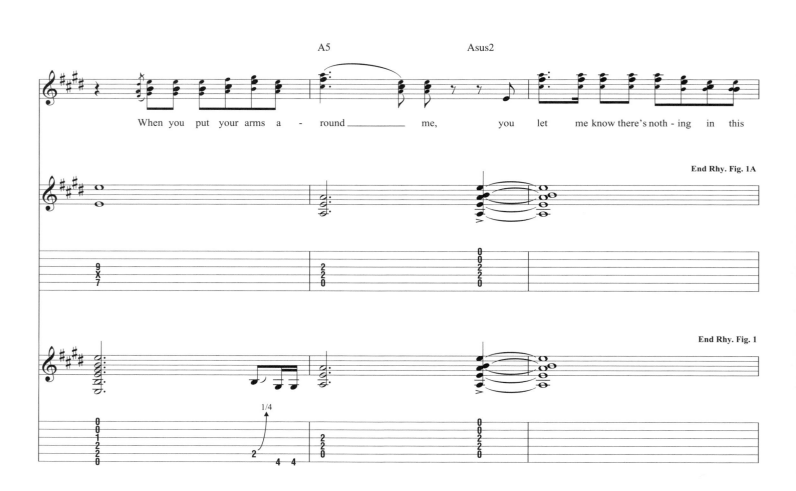

When you put your arms a - round ___ me, you let me know there's noth - ing in this

End Rhy. Fig. 1A

End Rhy. Fig. 1

two steps back. I could-n't walk a straight line ___ e - ven if I want-ed to. ___

Mm, hmm. _ I wan-na love some-bod-y, love _

Guitar Solo

Gtr. 4 tacet

E5

*Composite arrangement

Asus2

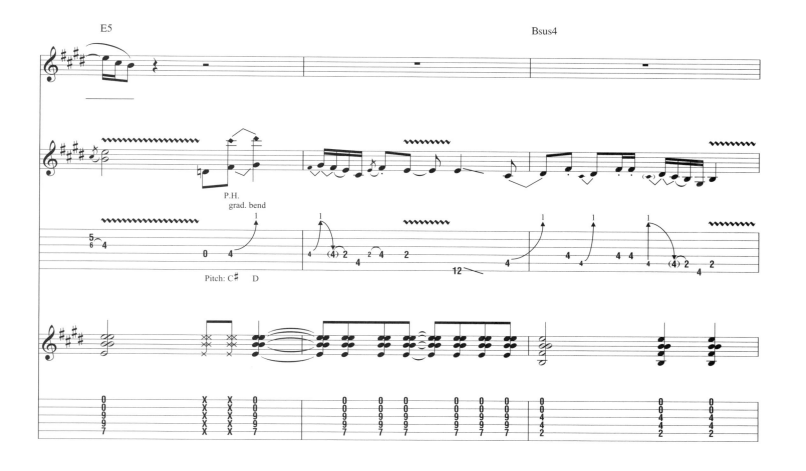

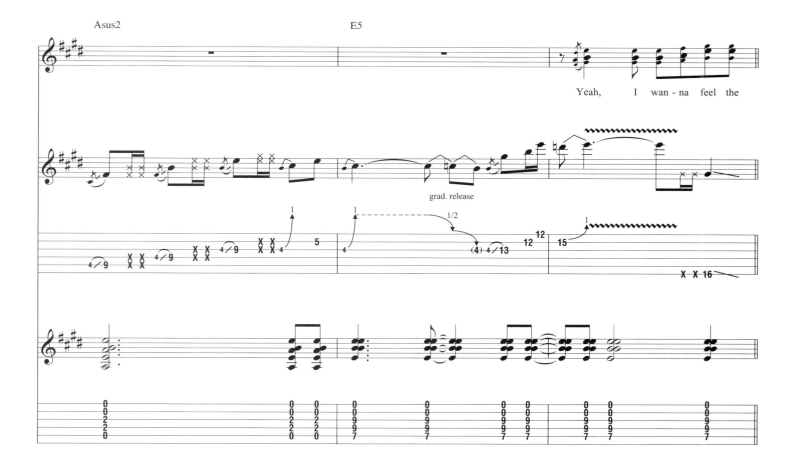

Chorus

Gtrs. 3 & 5: w/ Rhy. Fig. 1
Gtr. 4: w/ Rhy. Fig. 1A
Gtr. 8 tacet

sun - shine   shin - ing down on me and you.

When you put your arms a - round _____ me,   well, ba - by, there ain't noth - ing in this

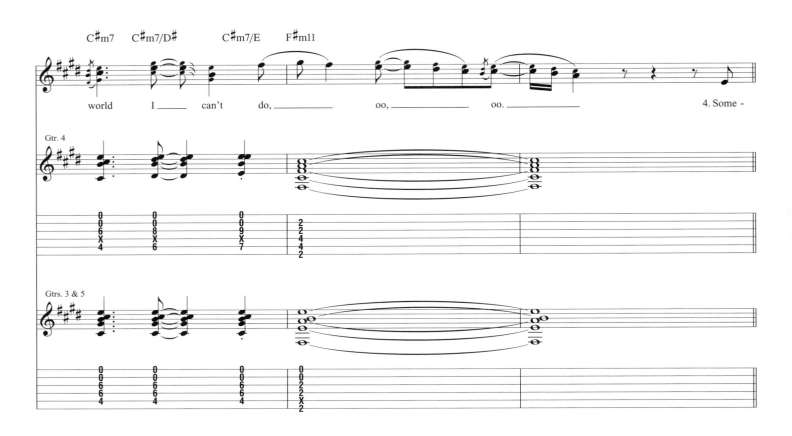

world I ___ can't do, _____ oo, _____ oo. _____   4. Some -

Verse

Gtrs. 4 & 5 tacet

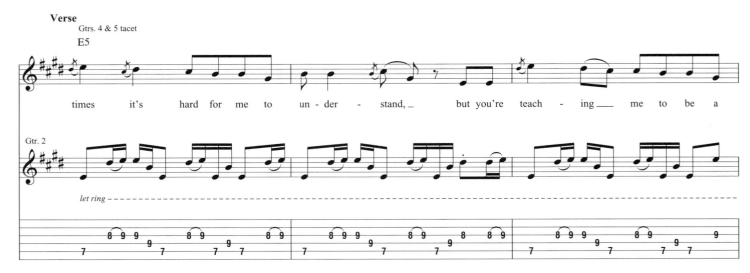

times it's hard for me to un - der - stand, _ but you're teach - ing ___ me to be a

bet - ter man.__ I don't want to take this life for grant - ed like I used to __ do.__

Gtr. 4

**Vol. swells

Gtr. 2

let ring -

Gtr. 3

*Vol. swells

Gtr. 5: w/ Riff B

Gtr. 4 tacet
Gtr. 5: w/ Riff C (2 times)

E5   B5

__ No, no. I wan - na love some - bod - y, love __

Riff D

let ring -

Gtr. 1 tacet

And I wan-na love some - bod - y love ___ some - bod - y like you, ___

*Composite arrangement

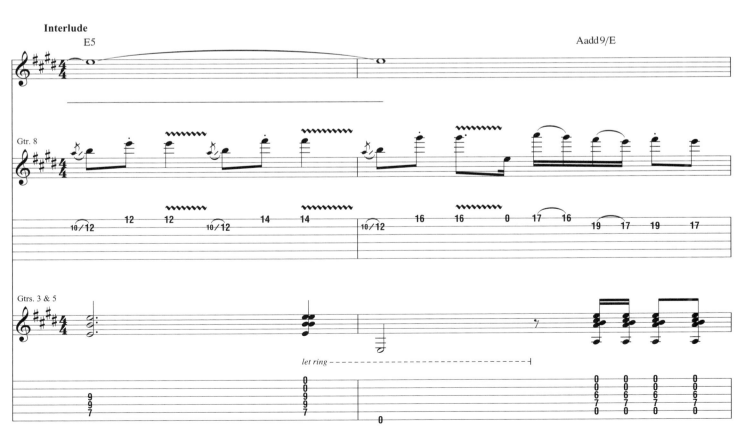

Interlude

let ring -

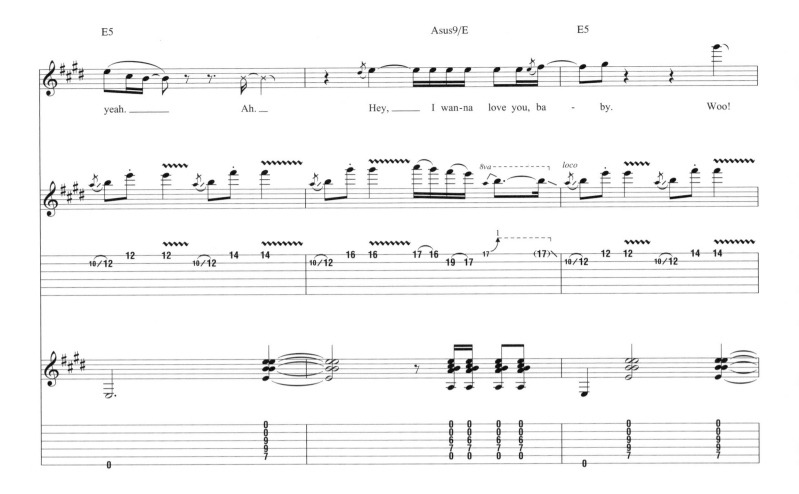

yeah. _____   Ah. _   Hey, _____ I wan-na love you, ba - by.   Woo!

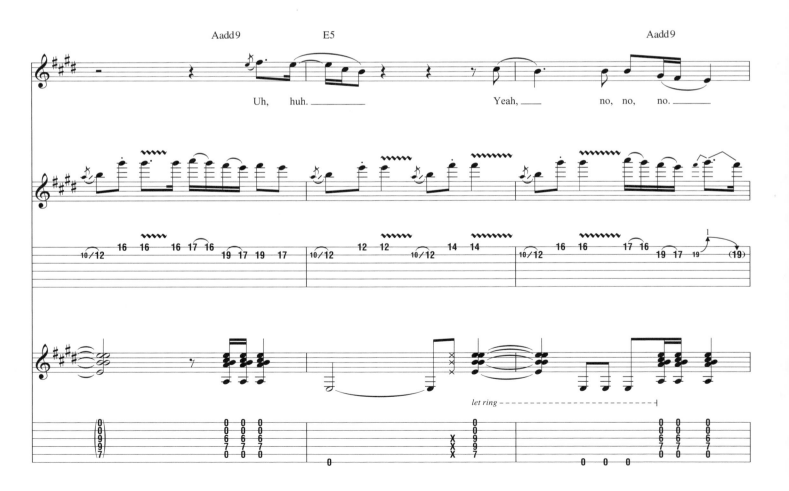

Uh, huh. _____   Yeah, _____ no, no, no. _____

D5   E5

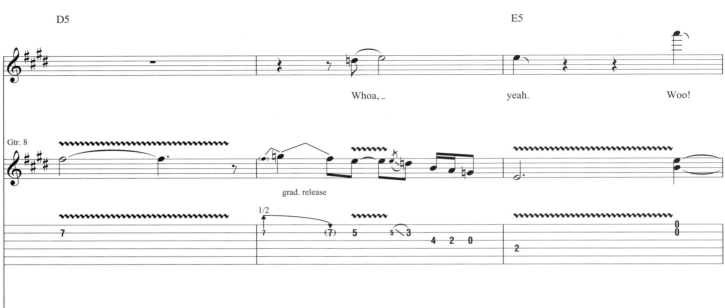

Whoa, _____   yeah.   Woo!

Gtr. 8

grad. release

*Gtrs. 3 & 5

f

*Composite arrangement

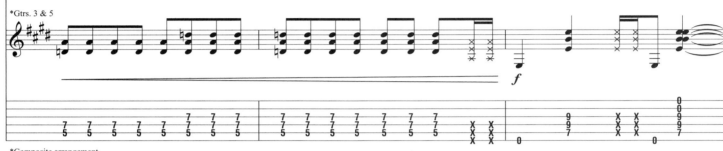

D⁶₉/E   Asus2

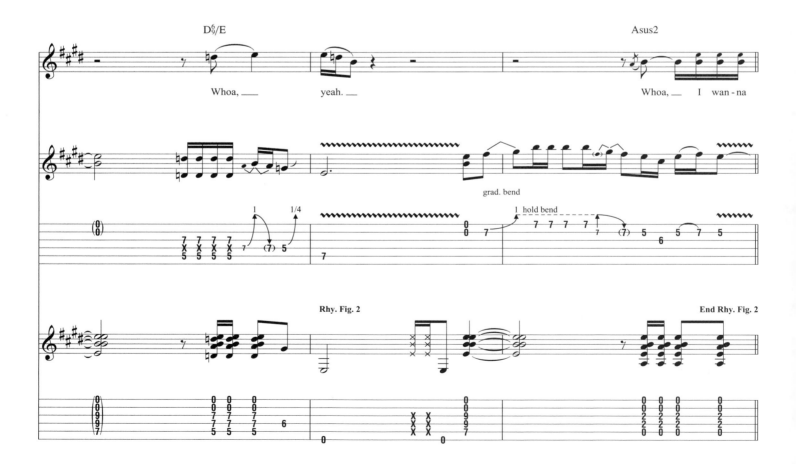

Whoa, _____   yeah. _____   Whoa, ___ I wan-na

grad. bend

1 hold bend

Rhy. Fig. 2   End Rhy. Fig. 2

Outro
Gtr. 2: w/ Riff A (till fade)
Gtrs. 3 & 5: w/ Rhy. Fig. 2 (till fade)

153

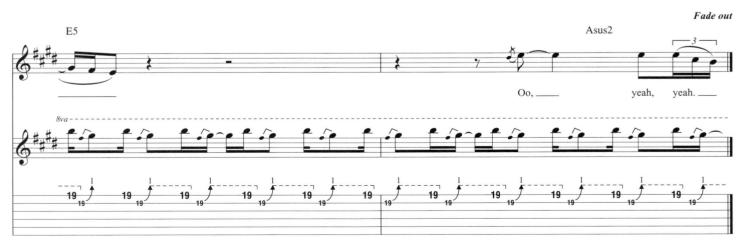

from *Love, Pain & The Whole Crazy Thing*

Stupid Boy

Words and Music by Sarah Buxton, Dave Berg and Deanna Bryant

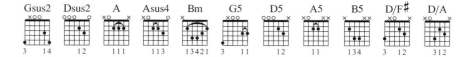

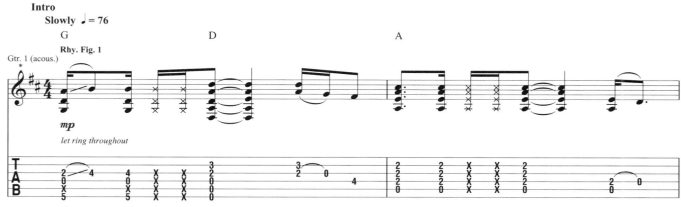

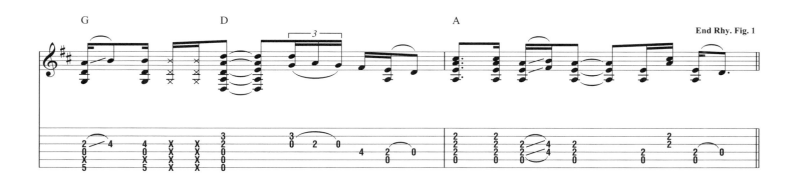

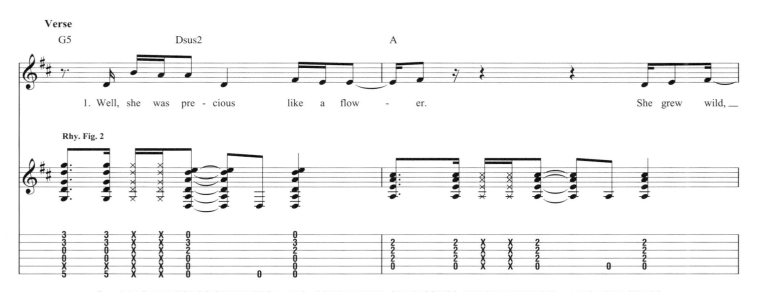

Gtr. 2: w/ Riff A

Gsus2   Dsus2   Asus4

it's like hold - in' back ___ the wind. _____ She laid ___

Gtr. 3 (elec.)

p

w/ dist.

Chorus

Gsus2   Dsus2   A   Asus4   A

Rhy. Fig. 3

___ her heart ___ and soul ___ right in your hands, _____   and you stole ___

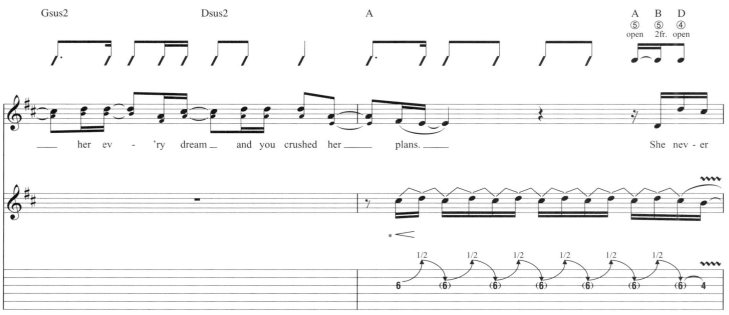

Gsus2   Dsus2   A   A B D
                                                                    ⑤ ⑤ ④
                                                                    open 2fr. open

___ her ev - 'ry dream ___ and you crushed her _____ plans. _____   She nev - er

*Vol. swell

157

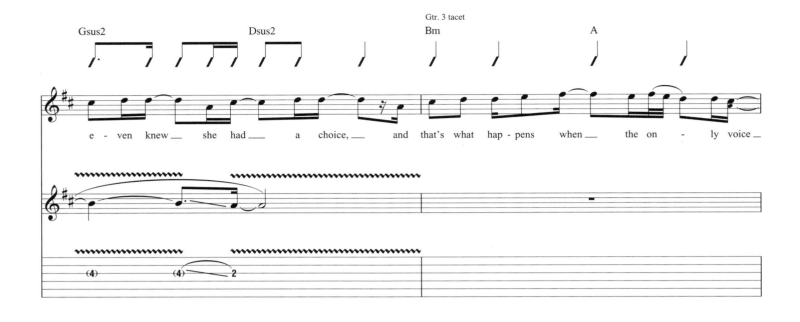

e - ven knew ___ she had ___ a choice, ___ and that's what hap - pens when ___ the on - ly voice ___

___ she hears ___ is tell - ing her ___ she ___ can't. _____ Stu - pid boy, ___

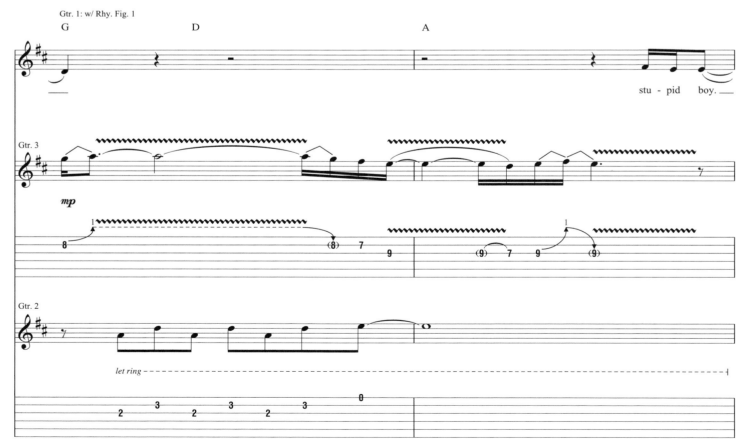

stu - pid boy. ___

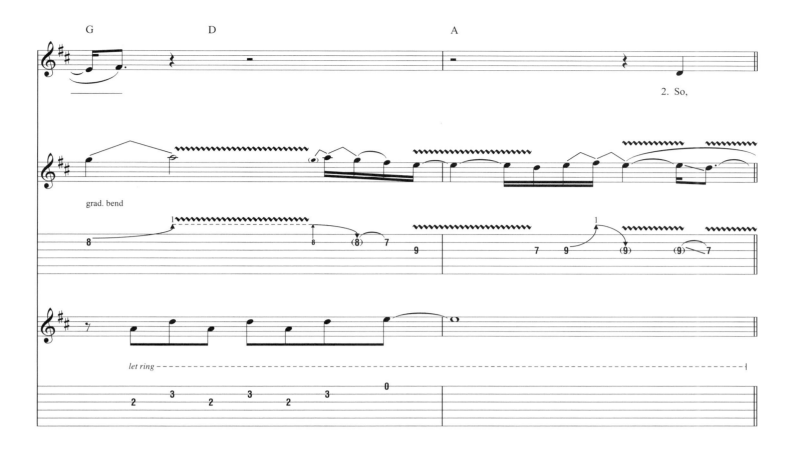

Verse

Gtr. 1: w/ Rhy. Fig. 2

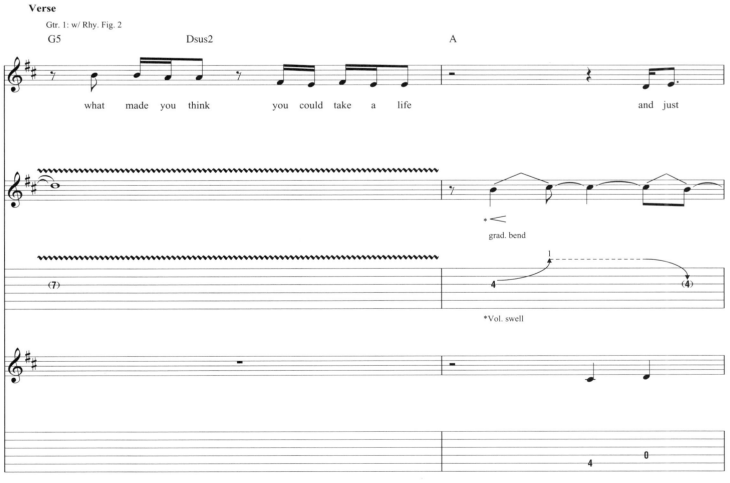

what made you think you could take a life and just

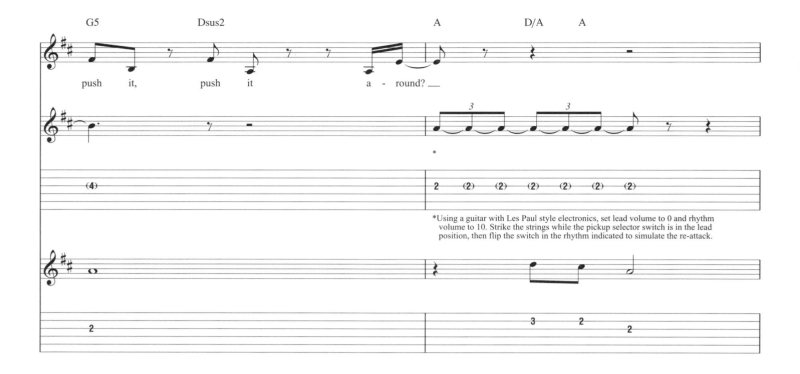

push it, push it a - round? __

*Using a guitar with Les Paul style electronics, set lead volume to 0 and rhythm volume to 10. Strike the strings while the pickup selector switch is in the lead position, then flip the switch in the rhythm indicated to simulate the re-attack.

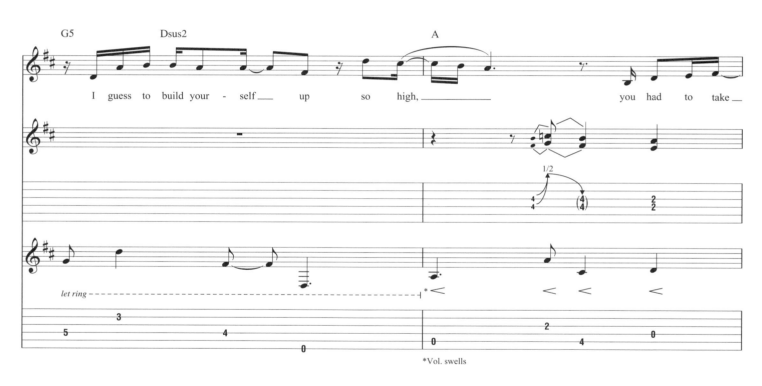

I guess to build your-self __ up so high, _____ you had to take __

*Vol. swells

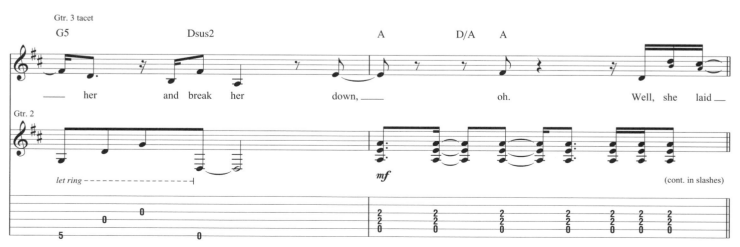

Gtr. 3 tacet

__ her and break her down, __ oh. Well, she laid __

Gtr. 2

let ring ------------------

mf

(cont. in slashes)

160

Chorus

her heart ___ and soul ___ right in your hands, ___ and you stole ___

her ev - 'ry dream ___ and you crushed her ___ plans. ___ She nev - er

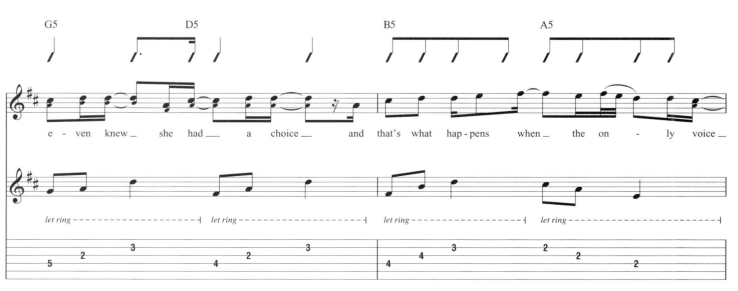

e - ven knew ___ she had ___ a choice ___ and that's what hap - pens when ___ the on - ly voice ___

she was ____   long gone, ____ long ____ gone. ____

Oh, ____   she's ____ gone. ____

Gone, gone.

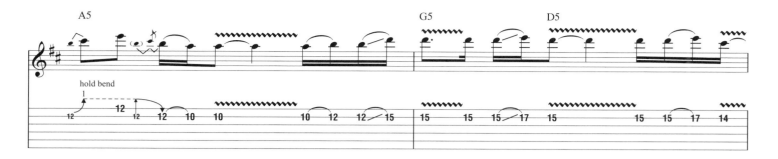

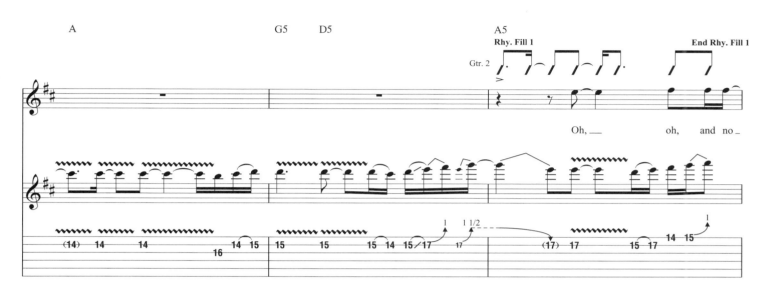

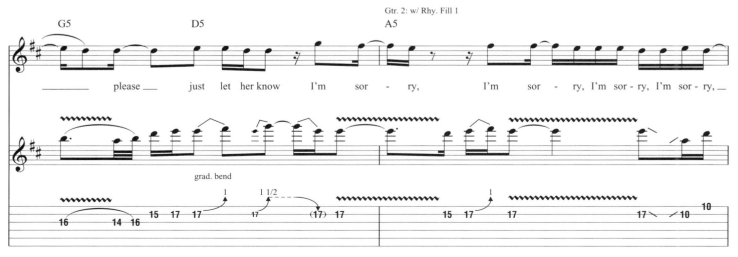

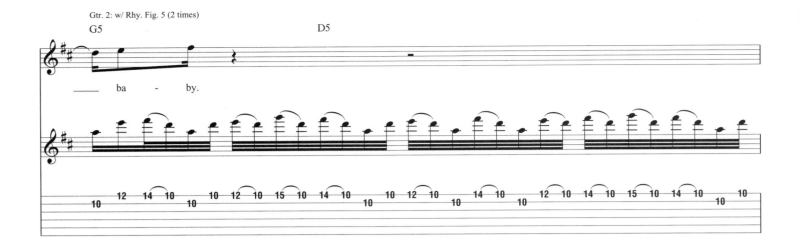

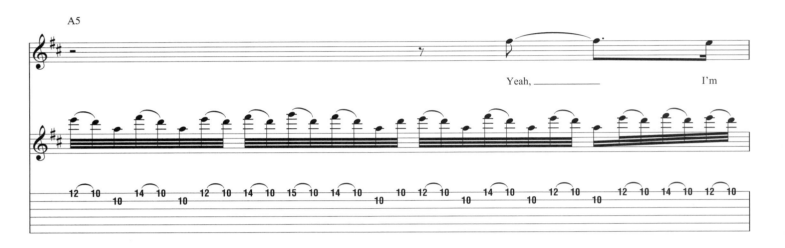

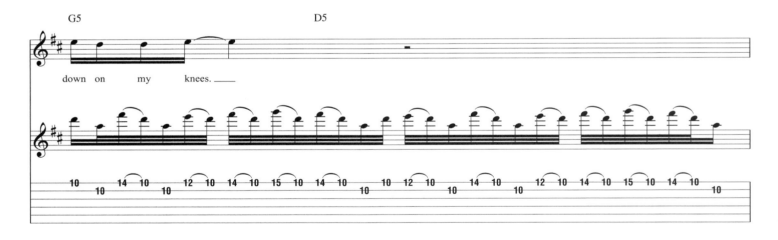

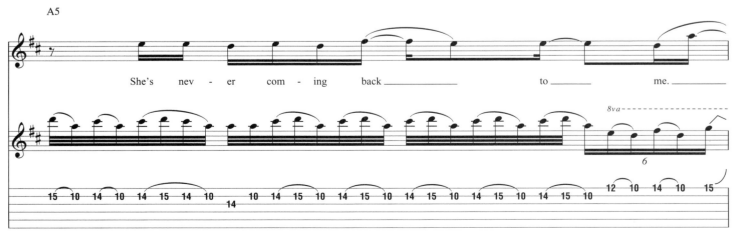

from *Defying Gravity*

'Til Summer Comes Around

Words and Music by Monty Powell and Keith Urban

†Chord symbols reflect overall harmony.
†††Delay set for eighth-note regeneration w/ 1 repeat.

Verse

Gtr. 1 tacet

Am   F   G

1. An - oth - er long sum - mer's come and _____ gone.

Gtr. 2

Gtr. 3

let ring - *let ring* - - - - - - - - - - - - - -

Am   F   G   Am   F

I don't know why ___ it al - ways ___ ends this way. ___ The board-walk's qui-et and the car-ni-val rides ___

Gtr. 3

*<

*Vol. swell

G   Fsus2   G5

are as emp-ty as my bro - ken _ heart, _ to - night. ___ But I

Gtr. 2   **Riff A**   **End Riff A**

Gtr. 3

let ring - *let ring* -

172

Chorus

Gtr. 2 tacet

Close my eyes __ and one more time we're spin-ning a - round _____ and you're hold-ing on tight - ly. The

words came out __ I kissed your mouth, no Fourth __ of Ju - ly __ has ev - er burned so __ bright - ly. You

Verse

Gtrs. 1 & 2 tacet
Gtr. 5: w/ Rhy. Fig. 1 (4 times)

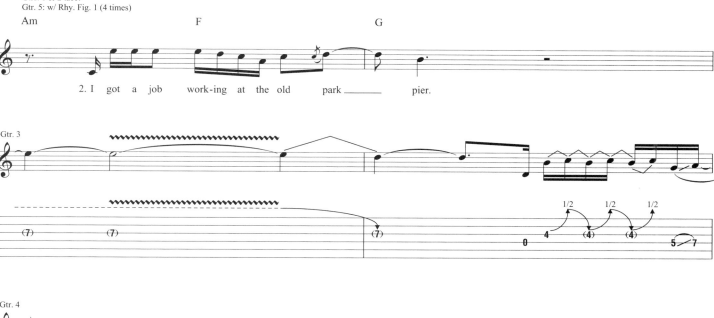

2. I got a job work-ing at the old park _____ pier.

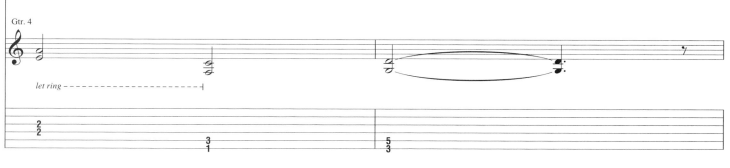

And ev - 'ry sum - mer now, _ for five ___ long years. _ I

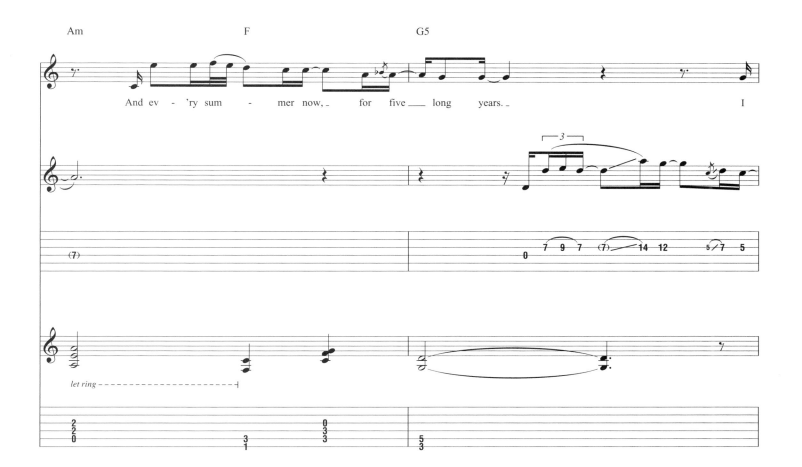

*See top of first page of song for chord diagrams pertaining to rhythm slashes.

180

181

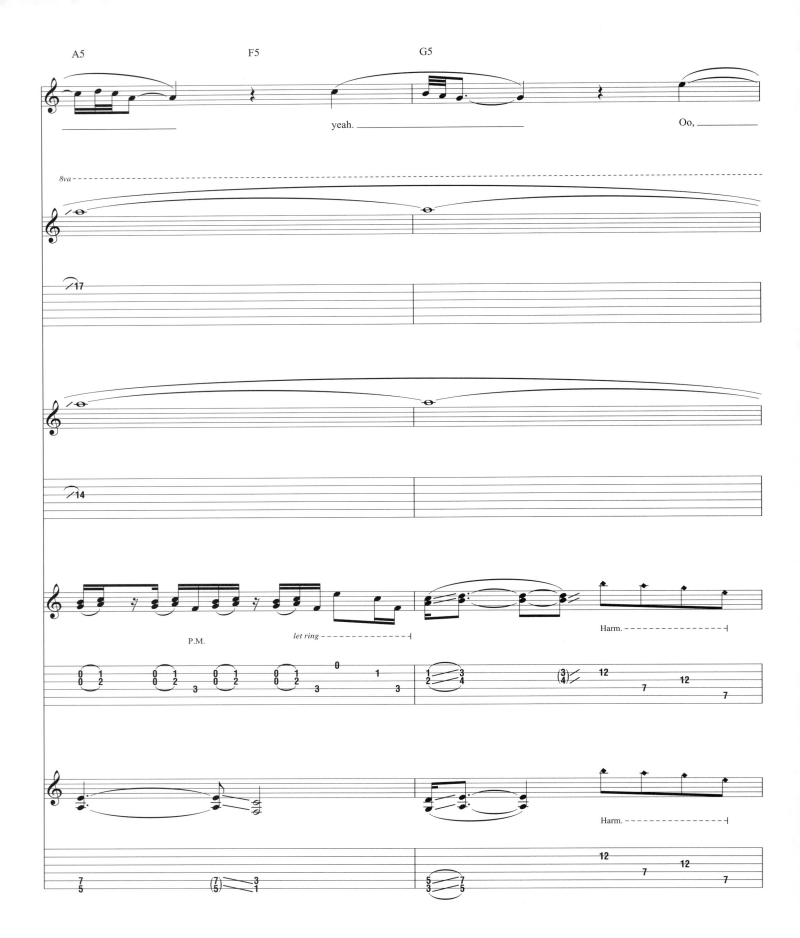

Gtrs. 1 & 2: w/ Riffs B & B1 (till fade)

a - round, and it comes a - round. Hoo, hoo, hoo,

hoo, hoo. Hoo, hoo, hoo,

189

You'll Think of Me

Words and Music by Ty Lacy, Dennis Matkosky and Darrell Brown

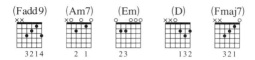

Gtr. 1: Capo II

Gtr. 2: Drop D tuning:
(low to high) D-A-D-G-B-E

Intro
Moderately slow ♩ = 88

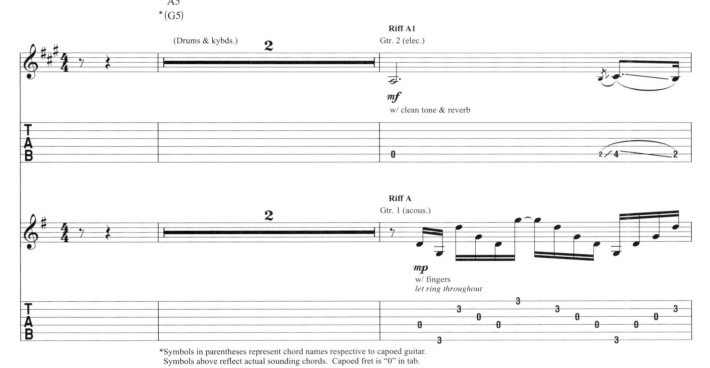

*Symbols in parentheses represent chord names respective to capoed guitar.
Symbols above reflect actual sounding chords. Capoed fret is "0" in tab.

thoughts of us ___ kept keep - ing me ___ a - wake. ___

Pre-Chorus

Bm7
(Am7)

F#m7
(Em7)

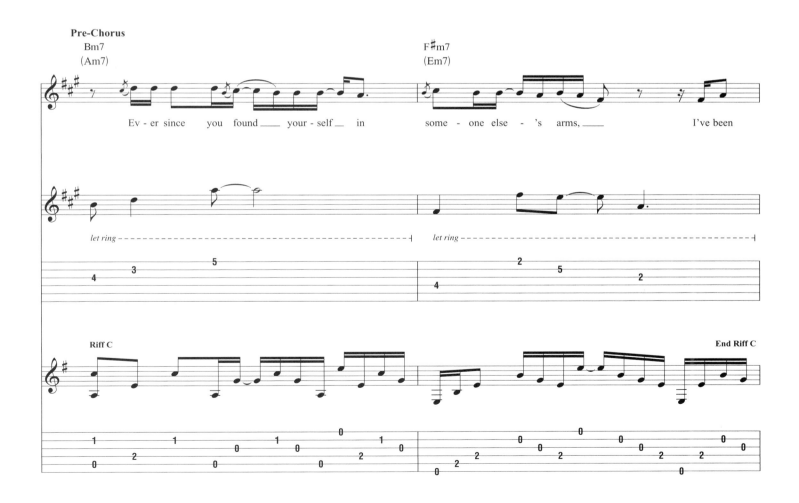

Ev - er since you found ___ your - self ___ in some - one else - 's arms, ___ I've been

'em. Take your space and take your rea - sons. But you'll think of me.

And take your cat and leave my sweat-er, 'cause we have noth - in' left to weath-

Verse

Gtr. 1: w/ Riff B
Gtr. 3 tacet

2. I went out driv-ing, try'n' to clear ___ my head. ___   I tried to sweep out all ___ the ru-ins that my ___

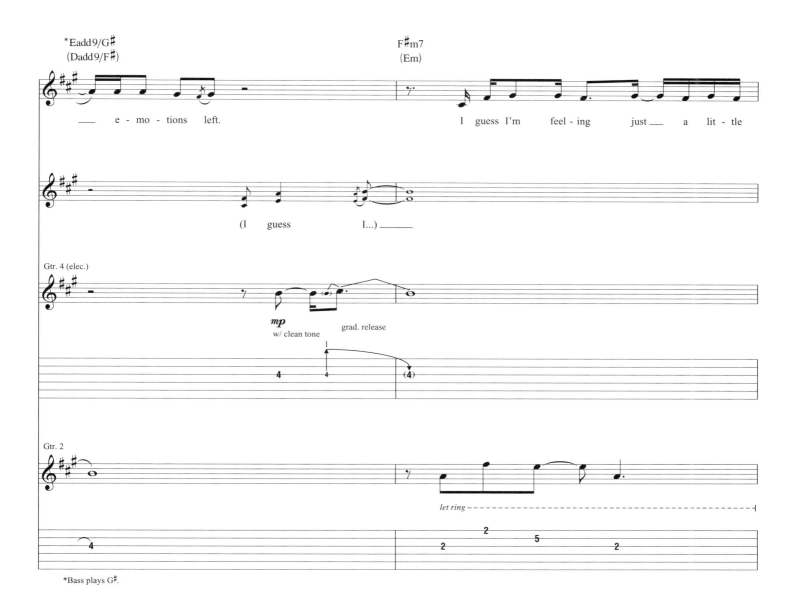

___ e - mo - tions left.   I guess I'm feel - ing just ___ a lit - tle

(I guess I...) ___

Gtr. 4 (elec.)

mp
w/ clean tone   grad. release

Gtr. 2

let ring

*Bass plays G♯.

-er. In fact, I'll feel a whole lot bet-ter. But you'll think of me.

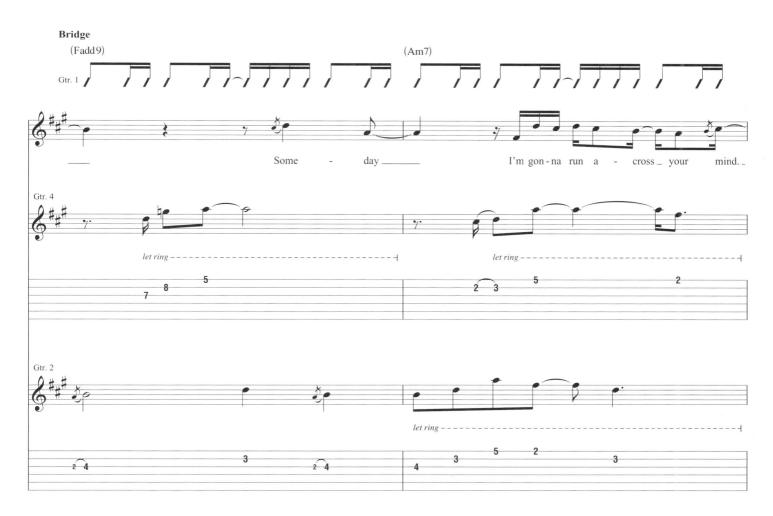

Bridge

Some - day I'm gon-na run a - cross your mind.

But don't wor-ry, I'll __ be fine. ___ I'm gon-na be al - right. __

(Be al - right.) __

While you're sleep - ing with __ your pride, ___ wish-ing I could hold __ you __

(Em)   (Fmaj7)

(cont. in notation)

___ tight, I'll be ___ o - ver you ___ and on ___ with my ___ life. _____

Breakdown-Chorus

Gtrs. 2 & 4 tacet

A5   Esus2

(G5)   (Dsus2)

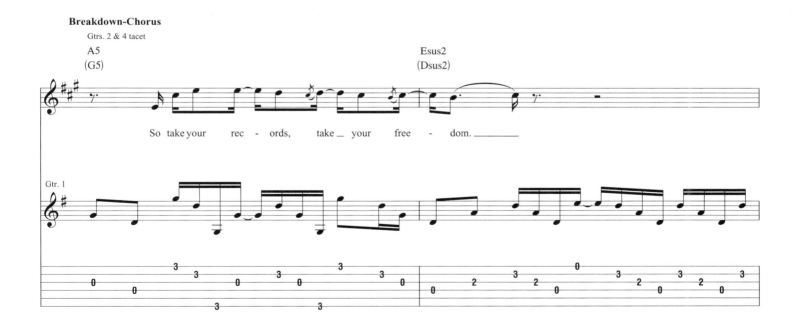

So take your rec - ords, take ___ your free - dom. _____

Gtr. 1

Chorus
Gtr. 1: w/ Riff D

*Bass plays G♯.

205

206

Outro

*Gtr. 1: w/ Riff A (5 times)
Gtr. 2: w/ Riff A1 (2 times)

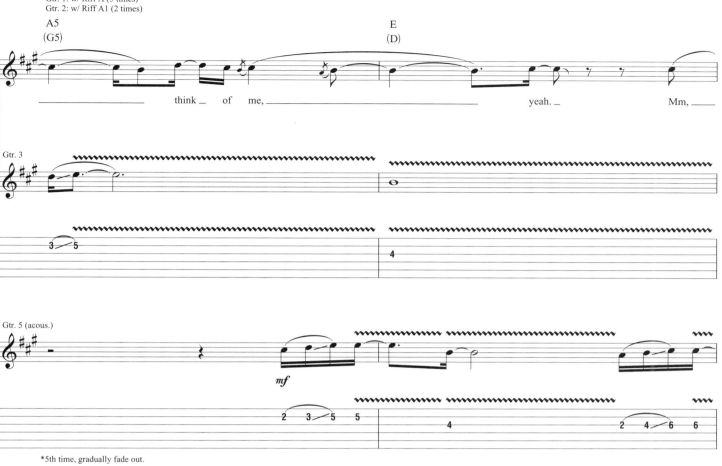

think ___ of me, _____ yeah. ___ Mm, _____

*5th time, gradually fade out.

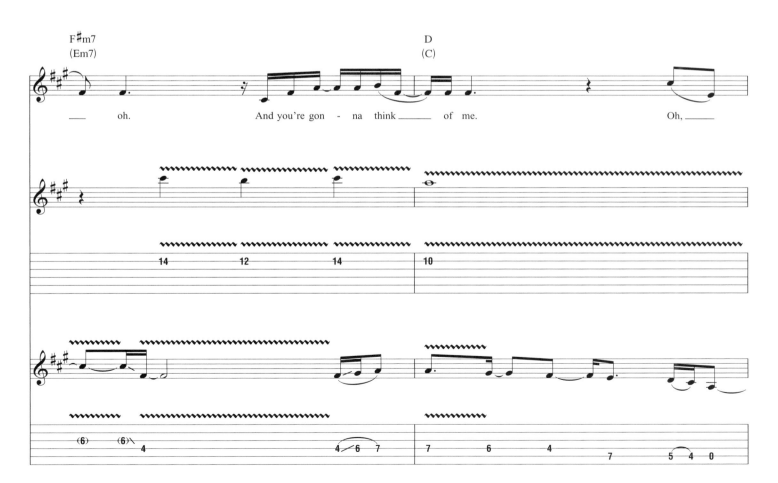

___ oh. And you're gon - na think _____ of me. Oh, _____

207

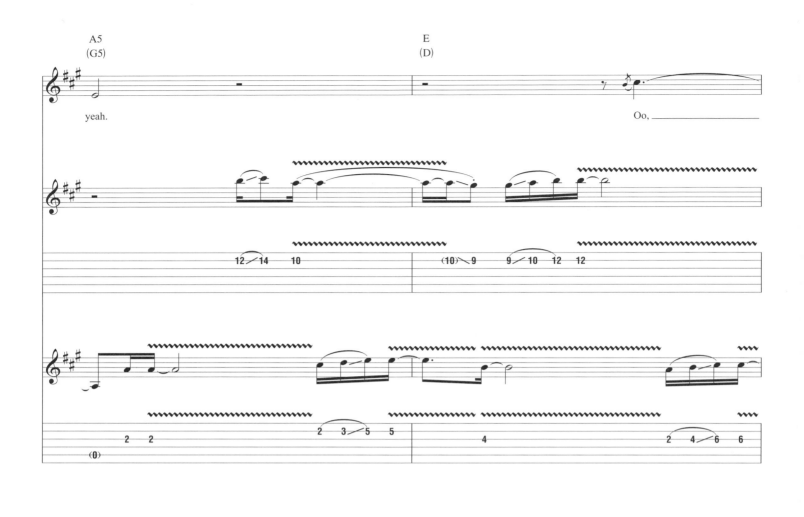

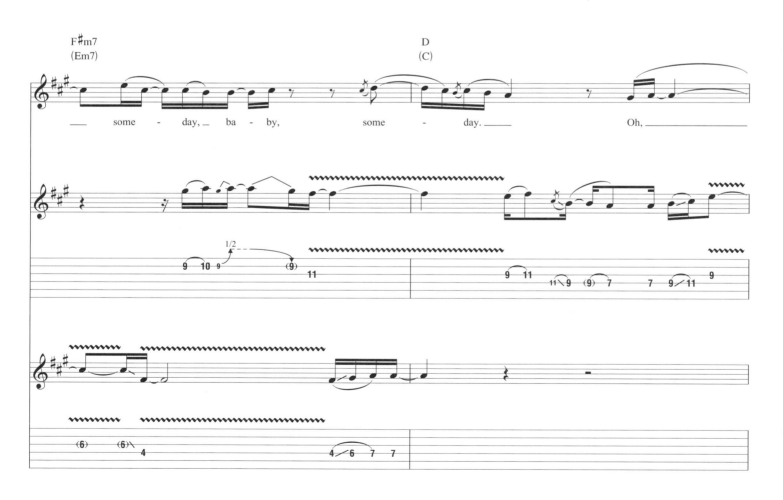

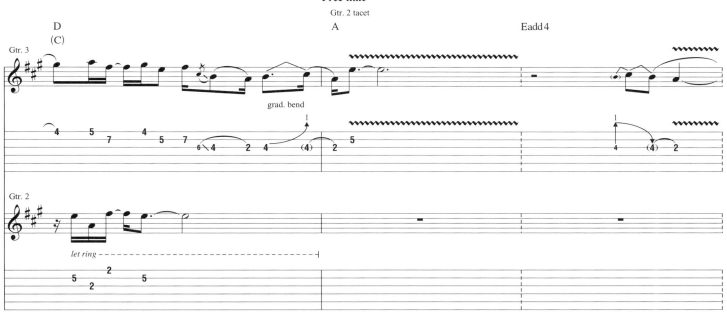

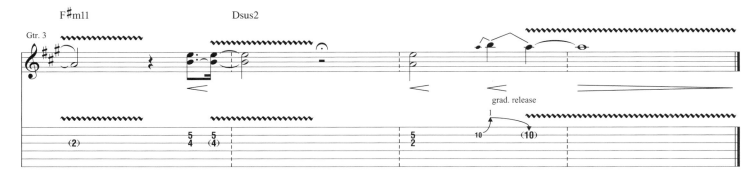

GUITAR NOTATION LEGEND

Guitar music can be notated three different ways: on a *musical staff*, in *tablature*, and in *rhythm slashes*.

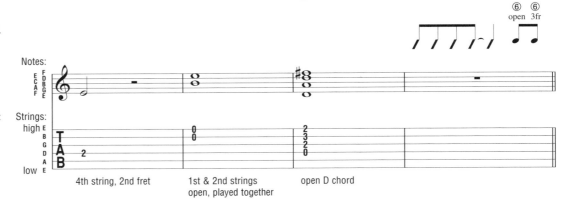

RHYTHM SLASHES are written above the staff. Strum chords in the rhythm indicated. Use the chord diagrams found at the top of the first page of the transcription for the appropriate chord voicings. Round noteheads indicate single notes.

THE MUSICAL STAFF shows pitches and rhythms and is divided by bar lines into measures. Pitches are named after the first seven letters of the alphabet.

TABLATURE graphically represents the guitar fingerboard. Each horizontal line represents a string, and each number represents a fret.

4th string, 2nd fret   1st & 2nd strings open, played together   open D chord

Definitions for Special Guitar Notation

HALF-STEP BEND: Strike the note and bend up 1/2 step.

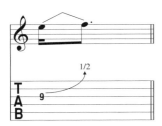

BEND AND RELEASE: Strike the note and bend up as indicated, then release back to the original note. Only the first note is struck.

VIBRATO: The string is vibrated by rapidly bending and releasing the note with the fretting hand.

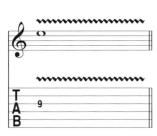

LEGATO SLIDE: Strike the first note and then slide the same fret-hand finger up or down to the second note. The second note is not struck.

WHOLE-STEP BEND: Strike the note and bend up one step.

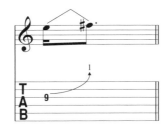

PRE-BEND: Bend the note as indicated, then strike it.

WIDE VIBRATO: The pitch is varied to a greater degree by vibrating with the fretting hand.

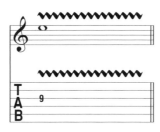

SHIFT SLIDE: Same as legato slide, except the second note is struck.

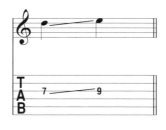

GRACE NOTE BEND: Strike the note and immediately bend up as indicated.

PRE-BEND AND RELEASE: Bend the note as indicated. Strike it and release the bend back to the original note.

HAMMER-ON: Strike the first (lower) note with one finger, then sound the higher note (on the same string) with another finger by fretting it without picking.

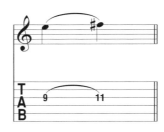

TRILL: Very rapidly alternate between the notes indicated by continuously hammering on and pulling off.

SLIGHT (MICROTONE) BEND: Strike the note and bend up 1/4 step.

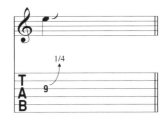

UNISON BEND: Strike the two notes simultaneously and bend the lower note up to the pitch of the higher.

PULL-OFF: Place both fingers on the notes to be sounded. Strike the first note and without picking, pull the finger off to sound the second (lower) note.

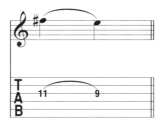

TAPPING: Hammer ("tap") the fret indicated with the pick-hand index or middle finger and pull off to the note fretted by the fret hand.

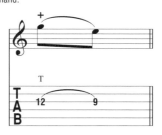

NATURAL HARMONIC: Strike the note while the fret-hand lightly touches the string directly over the fret indicated.

PINCH HARMONIC: The note is fretted normally and a harmonic is produced by adding the edge of the thumb or the tip of the index finger of the pick hand to the normal pick attack.

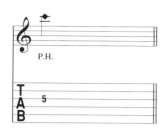

HARP HARMONIC: The note is fretted normally and a harmonic is produced by gently resting the pick hand's index finger directly above the indicated fret (in parentheses) while the pick hand's thumb or pick assists by plucking the appropriate string.

PICK SCRAPE: The edge of the pick is rubbed down (or up) the string, producing a scratchy sound.

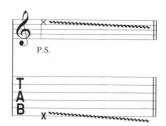

MUFFLED STRINGS: A percussive sound is produced by laying the fret hand across the string(s) without depressing, and striking them with the pick hand.

PALM MUTING: The note is partially muted by the pick hand lightly touching the string(s) just before the bridge.

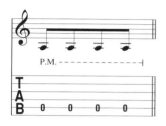

RAKE: Drag the pick across the strings indicated with a single motion.

TREMOLO PICKING: The note is picked as rapidly and continuously as possible.

ARPEGGIATE: Play the notes of the chord indicated by quickly rolling them from bottom to top.

VIBRATO BAR DIVE AND RETURN: The pitch of the note or chord is dropped a specified number of steps (in rhythm), then returned to the original pitch.

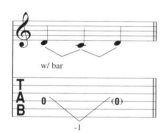

VIBRATO BAR SCOOP: Depress the bar just before striking the note, then quickly release the bar.

VIBRATO BAR DIP: Strike the note and then immediately drop a specified number of steps, then release back to the original pitch.

Additional Musical Definitions

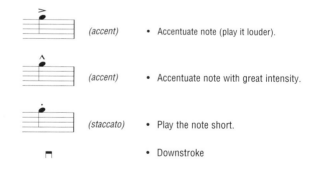

(accent) • Accentuate note (play it louder).

(accent) • Accentuate note with great intensity.

(staccato) • Play the note short.

• Downstroke

V • Upstroke

Rhy. Fig. • Label used to recall a recurring accompaniment pattern (usually chordal).

Riff • Label used to recall composed, melodic lines (usually single notes) which recur.

Fill • Label used to identify a brief melodic figure which is to be inserted into the arrangement.

Rhy. Fill • A chordal version of a Fill.

tacet • Instrument is silent (drops out).

D.S. al Coda • Go back to the sign (%), then play until the measure marked "*To Coda*," then skip to the section labelled "**Coda**."

D.C. al Fine • Go back to the beginning of the song and play until the measure marked "*Fine*" (end).

• Repeat measures between signs.

• When a repeated section has different endings, play the first ending only the first time and the second ending only the second time.

NOTE: Tablature numbers in parentheses mean:
   1. The note is being sustained over a system (note in standard notation is tied), or
   2. The note is sustained, but a new articulation (such as a hammer-on, pull-off, slide or vibrato) begins, or
   3. The note is a barely audible "ghost" note (note in standard notation is also in parentheses).

GUITAR RECORDED VERSIONS®

AUTHENTIC TRANSCRIPTIONS WITH NOTES AND TABLATURE

Guitar Recorded Versions® are note-for-note transcriptions of guitar music taken directly off recordings. This series, one of the most popular in print today, features some of the greatest guitar players and groups from blues and rock to country and jazz.

Guitar Recorded Versions are transcribed by the best transcribers in the business. Every book contains notes and tablature. Visit **www.halleonard.com** for our complete selection.

14041344 The Definitive AC/DC Songbook	$39.99
00690016 The Will Ackerman Collection	$19.95
00690501 Bryan Adams – Greatest Hits	$19.95
00692015 Aerosmith – Greatest Hits	$22.95
00690603 Aerosmith – O Yeah! (Ultimate Hits)	$24.95
00690147 Aerosmith – Rocks	$19.95
00690178 Alice in Chains – Acoustic	$19.95
00694865 Alice in Chains – Dirt	$19.95
00660225 Alice in Chains – Facelift	$19.95
00694925 Alice in Chains – Jar of Flies/Sap	$19.95
00690387 Alice in Chains – Nothing Safe: Best of the Box	$19.95
00690899 All That Remains – The Fall of Ideals	$22.99
00691056 All That Remains – For We Are Many	$22.99
00690980 All That Remains – Overcome	$22.99
00690812 All-American Rejects – Move Along	$19.95
00694932 Allman Brothers Band – Definitive Collection for Guitar Volume 1	$24.95
00694933 Allman Brothers Band – Definitive Collection for Guitar Volume 2	$24.95
00694934 Allman Brothers Band – Definitive Collection for Guitar Volume 3	$24.95
00690958 Duane Allman Guitar Anthology	$24.99
00691071 Alter Bridge – AB III	$22.99
00690945 Alter Bridge – Blackbird	$22.99
00690755 Alter Bridge – One Day Remains	$22.99
00690571 Trey Anastasio	$19.95
00114564 As I Lay Dying – Awakened	$22.99
00690158 Chet Atkins – Almost Alone	$19.95
00694876 Chet Atkins – Contemporary Styles	$19.95
00694878 Chet Atkins – Vintage Fingerstyle	$19.95
00690609 Audioslave	$19.95
00690804 Audioslave – Out of Exile	$19.95
00690884 Audioslave – Revelations	$19.95
00690926 Avenged Sevenfold	$22.95
00690820 Avenged Sevenfold – City of Evil	$24.95
00123216 Avenged Sevenfold – Hail to the King	$22.99
00691065 Avenged Sevenfold – Waking the Fallen	$22.99
00694918 Randy Bachman Collection	$22.95
00690503 Beach Boys – Very Best of	$19.95
00694929 Beatles: 1962-1966	$24.99
00694930 Beatles: 1967-1970	$24.95
00690489 Beatles – 1	$24.99
00694880 Beatles – Abbey Road	$19.95
00691066 Beatles – Beatles for Sale	$22.99
00690110 Beatles – Book 1 (White Album)	$19.95
00690111 Beatles – Book 2 (White Album)	$19.95
00690902 Beatles – The Capitol Albums, Volume 1	$24.99
00694832 Beatles – For Acoustic Guitar	$22.99
00691031 Beatles – Help!	$19.99
00690482 Beatles – Let It Be	$17.95
00691067 Beatles – Meet the Beatles!	$22.99
00691068 Beatles – Please Please Me	$22.99
00694891 Beatles – Revolver	$19.95
00694914 Beatles – Rubber Soul	$22.99
00694863 Beatles – Sgt. Pepper's Lonely Hearts Club Band	$22.99
00110193 Beatles – Tomorrow Never Knows	$22.99
00691044 Jeff Beck – Best of Beck	$24.99
00690632 Beck – Sea Change	$19.95
00691041 Jeff Beck – Truth	$19.99
00694884 Best of George Benson	$19.95
00692385 Chuck Berry	$19.95
00690835 Billy Talent	$19.95
00690879 Billy Talent II	$19.95
00690149 Black Sabbath	$16.99
00690901 Best of Black Sabbath	$19.95
00691010 Black Sabbath – Heaven and Hell	$22.99
00690148 Black Sabbath – Master of Reality	$16.99
00690142 Black Sabbath – Paranoid	$16.99
14042759 Black Sabbath – 13	$19.99
00692200 Black Sabbath – We Sold Our Soul for Rock 'N' Roll	$19.95

00690389 blink-182 – Enema of the State	$19.95
00690831 blink-182 – Greatest Hits	$19.95
00691179 blink-182 – Neighborhoods	$22.99
00690523 blink-182 – Take Off Your Pants and Jacket	$19.95
00690028 Blue Oyster Cult – Cult Classics	$19.95
00690008 Bon Jovi – Cross Road	$19.95
00691074 Bon Jovi – Greatest Hits	$22.99
00690913 Boston	$19.95
00690829 Boston Guitar Collection	$19.99
00690491 Best of David Bowie	$19.95
00690583 Box Car Racer	$19.95
00691023 Breaking Benjamin – Dear Agony	$22.99
00690873 Breaking Benjamin – Phobia	$19.95
00690764 Breaking Benjamin – We Are Not Alone	$19.95
00690451 Jeff Buckley Collection	$24.95
00690957 Bullet for My Valentine – Scream Aim Fire	$22.99
00119629 Bullet for My Valentine – Temper Temper	$22.99
00690678 Best of Kenny Burrell	$19.95
00691077 Cage the Elephant – Thank You, Happy Birthday	$22.99
00691159 The Cars – Complete Greatest Hits	$22.99
00690261 Carter Family Collection	$19.95
00691079 Best of Johnny Cash	$22.99
00690043 Best of Cheap Trick	$19.95
00690171 Chicago – The Definitive Guitar Collection	$22.95
00691011 Chimaira Guitar Collection	$24.99
00690567 Charlie Christian – The Definitive Collection	$19.95
00101916 Eric Church – Chief	$22.99
00690590 Eric Clapton – Anthology	$29.95
00692391 Best of Eric Clapton – 2nd Edition	$22.95
00691055 Eric Clapton – Clapton	$22.99
00690936 Eric Clapton – Complete Clapton	$29.99
00690074 Eric Clapton – Cream of Clapton	$24.95
00690247 Eric Clapton – 461 Ocean Boulevard	$19.99
00690010 Eric Clapton – From the Cradle	$19.95
00690363 Eric Clapton – Just One Night	$24.99
00694873 Eric Clapton – Timepieces	$19.95
00694869 Eric Clapton – Unplugged	$22.95
00690415 Clapton Chronicles – Best of Eric Clapton	$18.95
00694896 John Mayall/Eric Clapton – Bluesbreakers	$19.95
00690162 Best of the Clash	$19.95
00690828 Coheed & Cambria – Good Apollo I'm Burning Star, IV, Vol. 1: From Fear Through the Eyes of Madness	$19.95
00690940 Coheed and Cambria – No World for Tomorrow	$19.95
00690494 Coldplay – Parachutes	$19.95
00690593 Coldplay – A Rush of Blood to the Head	$19.95
00690806 Coldplay – X & Y	$19.95
00690855 Best of Collective Soul	$19.95
00691091 The Best of Alice Cooper	$22.99
00694940 Counting Crows – August & Everything After	$19.95
00694840 Cream – Disraeli Gears	$19.95
00690285 Cream – Those Were the Days	$17.95
00690819 Best of Creedence Clearwater Revival	$22.95
00690648 The Very Best of Jim Croce	$19.95
00690572 Steve Cropper – Soul Man	$19.95
00690613 Best of Crosby, Stills & Nash	$22.99
00699521 The Cure – Greatest Hits	$24.95
00690637 Best of Dick Dale	$19.95
00690822 Best of Alex De Grassi	$19.95
00690967 Death Cab for Cutie – Narrow Stairs	$22.99
00690289 Best of Deep Purple	$19.99
00690288 Deep Purple – Machine Head	$17.99
00690784 Best of Def Leppard	$19.95
00694831 Derek and the Dominos – Layla & Other Assorted Love Songs	$22.95
00692240 Bo Diddley – Guitar Solos by Fred Sokolow	$19.99
00690384 Best of Ani DiFranco	$19.95
00690380 Ani DiFranco – Up Up Up Up Up Up	$19.95
00690979 Best of Dinosaur Jr.	$19.99
00690833 Private Investigations – Best of Dire Straits and Mark Knopfler	$24.95

00695382 Very Best of Dire Straits – Sultans of Swing	$22.95
00690250 Best of Duane Eddy	$16.95
00690909 Best of Tommy Emmanuel	$22.99
00690555 Best of Melissa Etheridge	$19.95
00690515 Extreme II – Pornograffitti	$19.95
00691009 Five Finger Death Punch	$19.99
00690664 Best of Fleetwood Mac	$19.95
00690870 Flyleaf	$19.95
00690808 Foo Fighters – In Your Honor	$19.95
00691115 Foo Fighters – Wasting Light	$22.99
00690805 Best of Robben Ford	$22.99
00690842 Best of Peter Frampton	$19.95
00694920 Best of Free	$19.95
00694807 Danny Gatton – 88 Elmira St.	$19.95
00690438 Genesis Guitar Anthology	$19.95
00690753 Best of Godsmack	$19.95
00120167 Godsmack	$19.95
00690338 Goo Goo Dolls – Dizzy Up the Girl	$19.95
00113073 Green Day – Uno	$21.99
00116846 Green Day – ¡Dos!	$21.99
00118259 Green Day – ¡Tré!	$21.99
00691190 Best of Peter Green	$19.99
00690927 Patty Griffin – Children Running Through	$19.95
00690591 Patty Griffin – Guitar Collection	$19.95
00690978 Guns N' Roses – Chinese Democracy	$24.99
00691027 Buddy Guy Anthology	$24.99
00694854 Buddy Guy – Damn Right, I've Got the Blues	$19.95
00690697 Best of Jim Hall	$19.95
00690840 Ben Harper – Both Sides of the Gun	$19.95
00691018 Ben Harper – Fight for Your Mind	$22.99
00690987 Ben Harper and Relentless7 – White Lies for Dark Times	$22.99
00694798 George Harrison Anthology	$19.95
00690841 Scott Henderson – Blues Guitar Collection	$19.95
00692930 Jimi Hendrix – Are You Experienced?	$24.95
00692931 Jimi Hendrix – Axis: Bold As Love	$22.95
00690304 Jimi Hendrix – Band of Gypsys	$24.99
00690608 Jimi Hendrix – Blue Wild Angel	$24.95
00694944 Jimi Hendrix – Blues	$24.95
00692932 Jimi Hendrix – Electric Ladyland	$24.95
00119619 Jimi Hendrix – People, Hell and Angels	$22.99
00690602 Jimi Hendrix – Smash Hits	$24.95
00691152 West Coast Seattle Boy: The Jimi Hendrix Anthology	$29.99
00691332 Jimi Hendrix – Winterland (Highlights)	$22.99
00690017 Jimi Hendrix – Woodstock	$24.95
00690843 H.I.M. – Dark Light	$19.95
00690869 Hinder – Extreme Behavior	$19.95
00660029 Buddy Holly	$22.99
00690793 John Lee Hooker Anthology	$24.99
00660169 John Lee Hooker – A Blues Legend	$19.95
00694905 Howlin' Wolf	$19.95
00690692 Very Best of Billy Idol	$19.95
00121961 Imagine Dragons – Night Visions	$22.99
00690688 Incubus – A Crow Left of the Murder	$19.95
00690136 Indigo Girls – 1200 Curfews	$22.95
00690790 Iron Maiden Anthology	$24.99
00691058 Iron Maiden – The Final Frontier	$22.99
00690887 Iron Maiden – A Matter of Life and Death	$24.95
00690730 Alan Jackson – Guitar Collection	$19.95
00694938 Elmore James – Master Electric Slide Guitar	$19.95
00690652 Best of Jane's Addiction	$19.95
00690684 Jethro Tull – Aqualung	$19.95
00690693 Jethro Tull Guitar Anthology	$22.99
00691182 Jethro Tull – Stand Up	$22.99
00690898 John 5 – The Devil Knows My Name	$22.95
00690814 John 5 – Songs for Sanity	$19.95
00690751 John 5 – Vertigo	$19.95
00694912 Eric Johnson – Ah Via Musicom	$19.95
00690660 Best of Eric Johnson	$22.99
00691076 Eric Johnson – Up Close	$22.99

    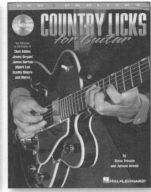

Guitar Instruction
Country Style!
from Hal Leonard

CHICKEN PICKIN' • *by Eric Halbig* **INCLUDES TAB**

This book provides a "bird's-eye-view" of the techniques and licks common to playing hot, country lead guitar! Covers over 100 hot country guitar licks: open-string licks, double-stop licks, scales, string bending, repetitive sequences, and chromatic licks. CD includes 99 demonstration tracks with each lick performed at two tempos.
00695599 Book/CD Pack...$16.95

COUNTRY CLASSICS FOR GUITAR • *arr. Fred Sokolow* **INCLUDES TAB**

30 favorites arranged for solo guitar, including: Always on My Mind • Blue Eyes Crying in the Rain • Crazy • Folsom Prison Blues • If You've Got the Money (I've Got the Time) • Make the World Go Away • Rocky Top • Walking the Floor over You • Your Cheatin' Heart • and more.
00699246...$14.95

FRETBOARD ROADMAPS – COUNTRY GUITAR **INCLUDES TAB**

The Essential Patterns That All the Pros Know and Use • by Fred Sokolow

This book/CD pack will teach you how to play lead and rhythm in the country style anywhere on the fretboard in any key. You'll play basic country progressions, boogie licks, steel licks, and other melodies and licks. You'll also learn a variety of lead guitar styles using moveable scale patterns, sliding scale patterns, chord-based licks, double-note licks, and more. The book features easy-to-follow diagrams and instructions for beginning, intermediate, and advanced players.
00695353 Book/CD Pack..$14.99

SONGBOOK
COUNTRY GUITAR BIBLE

Note-for-note transcriptions with tab for 35 country classics, all in one hefty collection! Includes: Ain't Goin' Down ('Til the Sun Comes Up) • Big Time • Blue Eyes Crying in the Rain • Boot Scootin' Boogie • Cannon Ball Rag • Friends in Low Places • I'm So Lonesome I Could Cry • Little Sister • My Baby Thinks He's a Train • T-R-O-U-B-L-E • Wildwood Flower • and more.
00690465 Guitar Recorded Versions $19.95

FOR MORE INFORMATION, SEE YOUR LOCAL MUSIC DEALER,
OR WRITE TO:

HAL•LEONARD® CORPORATION
7777 W. BLUEMOUND RD. P.O. BOX 13819 MILWAUKEE, WI 53213

COUNTRY LICKS FOR GUITAR **INCLUDES TAB**

by Steve Trovato and Jerome Arnold

This unique package examines the lead guitar licks of the masters of country guitar, such as Chet Atkins, Jimmy Bryant, James Burton, Albert Lee, Scotty Moore, and many others! The accompanying CD includes demonstrations of each lick at normal and slow speeds. The instruction covers single-string licks, pedal-steel licks, open-string licks, chord licks, rockabilly licks, funky country licks, tips on fingerings, phrasing, technique, theory, and application.
00695577 Book/CD Pack.............................. $17.99

COUNTRY SOLOS FOR GUITAR **INCLUDES TAB**

by Steve Trovato

This unique book/CD pack lets guitarists examine the solo styles of axe masters such as Chet Atkins, James Burton, Ray Flacke, Albert Lee, Scotty Moore, Roy Nichols, Jerry Reed and others. It covers techniques including hot banjo rolls, funky double stops, pedal-steel licks, open-string licks and more, in standard notation and tab with phrase-by-phrase performance notes. The CD includes full demonstrations and rhythm-only tracks.
00695448 Book/CD Pack............................. $17.95

RED-HOT COUNTRY GUITAR

by Michael Hawley

The complete guide to playing lead guitar in the styles of Pete Anderson, Danny Gatton, Albert Lee, Brent Mason, and more. Includes loads of red-hot licks, techniques, solos, theory and more.
00695831 Book/CD Pack...$17.95

25 GREAT COUNTRY GUITAR SOLOS **INCLUDES TAB**

by Dave Rubin

Provides solo transcriptions in notes & tab, lessons on how to play them, guitarist bios, equipment notes, photos, history, and much more. The CD contains full-band demos of every solo in the book. Songs include: Country Boy • Foggy Mountain Special • Folsom Prison Blues • Hellecaster Theme • Hello Mary Lou • I've Got a Tiger by the Tail • The Only Daddy That Will Walk the Line • Please, Please Baby • Sugarfoot Rag • and more.
00699926 Book/CD Pack...$19.99

Visit Hal Leonard Online at www.halleonard.com
Prices, contents, and availability subject to change without notice.

0113